THE SECRET HANDBOOK FOR

Perpetually Paralyzed PROCRASTINATING PACK RATS

anonymous

by Pamela Nudelman

Panacea
16300 Cypress Way
Los Gatos, California   95030
(408) 395-0552
panacea7@aol.com
www.packratsanonymous.com

Library of Congress Cataloging-In-Publication Data

Nudelman, Pamela
The secret handbook for perpetually paralyzed procrastinating pack rats anonymous
by Pamela Nudelman
First edition 1999
Revised edition 2001

ISBN 0-9666656-0-0

1. Clutter control. 2. Paperwork paralysis.
3. Organizing ideas. 4. Procrastination. 5. Pack rats.
6. Household management. 7. Self help.
I. Title.

Printed in the United States of America

I dedicate this book to my husband, Alan, who is my love, and to my children, Joshua, Jessica, Matthew and Adam, for they are my life.

Acknowledgments

I would like to acknowledge my clients and the hundreds of students who attended my classes for their support, appreciation and encouragement.

I would also like to thank Linda Zeidler for her inspiration and Markene Kruse-Smith for her contagious enthusiasm and astute editorial skill.

Preface

This book is written for anyone who's inundated with papers and assorted paraphernalia, and who seeks to gain better control of this aspect of their life.

It is my hope to help you become conscious of your present living habits and patterns. By understanding why you've save things, you'll be able to develop an intelligent plan to make better choices in the future.

You'll discover many clever ideas which can be easily incorporated into your daily routine to manage your home and office more efficiently. You'll realize how to make maximum use of your time and energy, regain control of your life, reduce stress and significantly enhance your self image.

Above all, you'll learn to create and use your own clever new ideas to achieve your goals and fulfill your dreams.

May this book enlighten and inspire all *Perpetually Paralyzed Procrastinating Pack Rats!*

TABLE OF CONTENTS (DISORGANIZED)

TABLE OF CONTENTS (ORGANIZED)

INTRODUCTION

British biologist and philosopher Thomas Huxley once noted, "Perhaps the most valuable result of all education is the ability to make yourself do the thing you have to do when it ought to be done whether you like it or not. It is the first lesson that ought to be learned, and however early a person's training begins, it is probably the last lesson a person learns thoroughly."

Let's face it. Picking up after yourself and others is not fun. It's a boring and often thankless job that needs to be done over and over again. If you don't do it consistently, things begin to pile up, making your home or office unsightly to look at, inconvenient to work in, difficult to retrieve things from and sometimes embarrassing to live in.

Think about the reasons you've put off doing what you know you should do. Perhaps you chose to do something else because it was more fun than the present task. Or maybe you preferred to do an easier job instead. Possibly you've deferred completing a project because another was more financially or psychologically rewarding.

When tasks are repeatedly avoided and postponed, they become increasingly negative aspects of your life. Every time you look at your unfinished projects you send yourself a message saying you've failed. As time passes, these black holes appear to grow and overwhelm you.

Let's say you neglected sending out a timely thank you or sympathy note. In addition to coping with the guilt of not writing the note, you realize that because of the lateness, even if you actually get around to doing it, you'll suffer the embarrassment of a tardy response. If you find it necessary to justify your delay with a suitable explanation, it might be mentally exhausting, emotionally taxing and socially embarrassing.

Perhaps you have difficulty processing paperwork – you might page through a stack of papers only to realize you've set them back down again in reverse order without shrinking the pile. After awhile, you toss them because they're obsolete or no longer of importance to you.

You might delay finishing a job because you continually categorize it as being less important than your other projects. It gets buried deeper and deeper, and you eventually lose interest and eliminate it from your project list.

Possibly you delay something because you want to do something else beforehand. These postponed tasks quickly clog the arteries of your living space and cripple your daily functions.

Maybe you spend your days going from one crisis to another. Meeting deadlines in the nick of time might give you a temporary sense of control, but it won't let you off the roller coaster of threatening catastrophe.

Perhaps you never have enough time. Each day has only twenty-four hours and, no matter how much you may try, you can't extend your day beyond that number. Something eventually has to give. You may need to reevaluate your lifestyle and prioritize your obligations.

Whether you've substituted what you should have addressed for things that were more entertaining, simple, lucrative or fulfilling, you've procrastinated. When you procrastinate putting papers and things in their proper place, they become layers, stacks, and mounds in your home or office. To retrieve specific items you have to take valuable time to search through the piles.

Even if you are able to remember where things are spatially – in a general vicinity – and able to locate them after a quick search, consider how much time you devote, on an annual basis, to recovering various objects. If your total time exceeds a working day or more, maybe you should devote that same block of time to getting organized right now. To save time, you need to create and maintain workable systems.

Have courage to address the disorganization that paralyzes your life. It's human nature to envision things worse than they actually are. The looming threat you imagine is probably a series of simple, manageable tasks.

It is said that in the year 333 B.C., Gordius' chariot's yoke was lashed to a pole by means of a knot with no visible ends. According to legend, only the new conqueror of Asia could undo the knot. Many tried to untie it, but it was Alexander the Great who solved the dilemma by simply slashing the knot with his sword.

Whether your Gordian knot is an area, room or number of rooms, understand that most everyone faces unraveling disorganization issues throughout their lifetime. Many people are able to remedy this situation and return order to their homes or offices without too much thought or trouble. For others, the journey is seemingly more difficult.

The shortest distance between two points is a straight line. If you want to efficiently solve your disorganization problem, this book will put you where you want to be – back in control again – by the most direct route.

It will help you understand why you save things, where things belong, how to organize and maintain your home or office, how to make better decisions and how you can stay motivated. It encompasses the thought processes and the actual systems I've used to organize my own home and office as well as those of scores of clients.

Like the Gordian knot, your state of disorganization might be a complex, intertwined mess which appears to be impossible to unravel. My solutions in the following pages deal with solving the problem of disorganization. I show you how to organize your possessions – step-by-step, item-by-item, room-by-room – in a swift yet simple fashion. I don't dwell on the fact that there's a paralyzing knot in your life. That's an established fact.

When you are ill, you see a doctor. He diagnoses you then prescribes treatment. Regardless of how many doctors you see or diagnoses and prescriptions you get, you probably won't get better unless you take your medicine. If you realize you're a procrastinator, you have already diagnosed yourself. To attain a healthier level of organization, read my prescription for success, take the medicine, and you'll soon be inspired to get up, get moving, recover – and be back in control again.

- Pamela Nudelman

THE
SECRET HANDBOOK
FOR
Perpetually Paralyzed
PROCRASTINATING
PACK RATS
Anonymous

THINKING
IT THROUGH

- CHAPTER I -

THINKING IT THROUGH

Perpetually Paralyzed

Occasionally, a person will delay addressing his or her clutter for so long that it will eventually grow to unrealistic proportions and cover vital storage and work areas, thereby rendering the person incapable of movement. Paralyzed.

> *I have been in offices and homes in which people have piles of mail, papers, receipts and files stacked in one big pile. It's rather amusing to hear people say that they know exactly where everything is as they frantically go rifling through it.*

When you know where your possessions are spatially you still have to spend time searching for them. Eventually, these items need to be addressed. The longer you procrastinate, the bigger your knot of disorganization grows. The minutes you spend looking for items add up to hours then soon become days of unnecessarily wasted time. Eliminate repeatedly forfeiting time retrieving buried items. Stop procrastinating and spend an equivalent of last year's lost time to get organized now.

Procrastinating Pack Rats

What exactly is a pack rat? Its a rodent! One that habitually collects and brings various debris into its nest. Like this small pest, many people find their behavior compulsive and soon out of control. When you constantly bring more and more things into your "nest" without the ability to distinguish the extraneous from the necessary, you eventually render your living space dysfunctional.

> *When I pointed out to an economics professor client that his 2,400 square-foot home had only 240 usable square feet, and that he was paying for heat, electricity, water, garbage, taxes and a mortgage on his shrunken house, he was more motivated to downsize his possessions and clear space for a better return on his investment.*

1

Achieving Your Goal

When you have a goal you are more apt to make progress. The more serious the goal the more motivated you are. Low-priority tasks tend to be stalled, overlooked or disregarded.

> *I often ask clients if they think their ancestors would have hunted and foraged for food with such determination if their lives hadn't depended upon it. Probably not.*

Put a high-priority label on your goals. Imagine having more time to:

- Enjoy family or friends more
- Develop new interests
- Increase leisure time
- Pursue a career
- Increase your self-esteem.

Reasons Why People Procrastinate

There are a multitude of reasons why people procrastinate but the most common ones include:

- It can wait
- It isn't an emergency
- Its low on your priority list
- It isn't important to you
- It isn't interesting to you
- It isn't fun to do
- There's something else you'd rather do
- Something else needs to be done beforehand
- You don't necessarily need it anymore
- You don't know if you even want it
- You don't know how to begin tackling it
- You're afraid of making a mistake
- You've convinced yourself you can't do it
- There are no consequences in not finishing it
- There is no recognition or reward in finishing it

Dramatic Reasons Why People Procrastinate

Scarlett O'Hara Postponement Preference - "I'll think of it all tomorrow . . . I can stand it then. Tomorrow, I'll think of some way . . . After all, tomorrow is another day."

Porky Pig Indecisive Dilemma - "Dddo I need it now? Will I need it later? I mmmight need it later. I'll just hold onto it for the time bbbeing. But where should I ppput it? I don't know. I'll just set it bbback down here. Here. Rrright here."

Twilight Zone Physiological Phobia -

> *I've witnessed some people who get physically ill just contemplating the act of straightening their messes. Does the thought process trigger a chemical reaction that causes them to become emotionally or physically ill? Is it the dust or merely the visualization of hard work? Or, in truth, are they searching for a plausible excuse to avoid a productive task? Only those entering the twilight zone know.*

Lizzie Borden Psycho Babble -

> *Exploring one's past for answers of deep-seated emotions which might be responsible for present day procrastination can be a costly as well as time-consuming activity. Is this another way of avoiding work? Would not the time be better spent confronting the task? Could the money be spent in a more productive way? Precisely what expectations did Lizzie's mother impose upon her in keeping her room neat?*

Beaver Cleaver Whining Complex - "Aw, gee, Wally. It's easy for you, but I can't do it. I just couldn't do it. Even if I tried, I couldn't. I'd be real embarrassed if everybody knew. Gosh, I'm sorry, Wally."

Dennis the Menace Naughty Syndrome - Running away on short little legs and screaming, "No! I won't do it! I won't do it! I don't wanna do it! I just won't do it!"

How Do I Stop Being Such a Pack Rat?

First and foremost, you have to understand *why* you save the things that you do. Then you have to know *where* to put them. Once you understand both concepts, it will be far easier to follow through and *just do it.*

From now on, you must ask yourself these two questions whenever you have something in your hand and are about to put it down:

- *"Why* am I saving this?" and
- *"Where* does this logically belong?"

If you put something away in the right place the first time then you won't have to:

- Inconvenience yourself by its presence
- Move it again and again
- Keep looking at it
- Feel guilty about its clutter

So many times people save things but don't know the proper place to put them. It's my belief that once you know where something belongs then you'll be more apt to put it there.

This book will help you get your life and home organized by giving you a plethora of reasons, rituals and clever ideas regarding WHY you need things and WHERE they belong.

UFOs

Be aware of the mysterious phenomenon of those harmless, little items you stack on counters, tables, washers, dryers, dressers and beds. They tend to quietly mutate and multiply, move into various boxes and containers, then eventually spread to the floor, down hallways and mysteriously appear in other rooms.

These parasitic Unidentified Floating Objects gradually and unobtrusively consume entire homes, thereby rendering the occupants paralyzed and catatonic. It is truly a sad state of affairs but, with exorcism by organization, can be properly remedied.

Vampires in Your Castle

By delaying decisions and holding onto things year after year, you will slowly be sucked dry of the life blood of your time, space and energy.

As the caretaker of your property, you will be compelled to cart your belongings around from residence to residence, from room to room. You will have to clean, dust and fix them. You'll be responsible for them and perhaps to them. You'll become a loyal, mindless servant to them uttering, "Yes, master. Yes, master."

You'll keep forfeiting room – valuable space, that could feasibly be used for other purposes. Your belongings will become larger and stronger. Their existence and preservation will become foremost in your mind. They'll consume you. Like vampires, your extra possessions will develop a life of their own and will eventually leave you drained. And, if you don't exorcise them from your life, they'll be with you forever.

Pinball Wizard

Think of your day as one big pinball game. Be one jump ahead of the game by keeping your eyes open and anticipating your next crisis.

Whenever you get out of the shower, make a cursory glance around to inventory its contents to ensure the next person will be provided with soap, shampoo, conditioner, razor, washcloth and towel.

Whenever you replace a light bulb or a battery, check to make sure you have an adequate supply on hand for future needs.

When you buy a package of invitations, also purchase a box of thank you notes. Keep the guests' name and address list inside the box so you promptly send your notes of appreciation.

Don't wait until a situation becomes an emergency before you resolve it. By being aware of your environment, foreseeing potential problems and responding quickly, you'll be able to keep yourself in the game, score points and not bottom out.

Why We Save Things

There are several reasons why people save necessary as well as unnecessary, extra, useless, unrelated and superfluous things:

Need is the best reason to save things. Some individuals, however, frequently misapply the term "need" to all their possessions.

Sentimentality is an admirable quality, but only in moderation. It can easily be carried to an extreme when left unchecked by collecting an overabundance of items that have little or no worth other than having belonged to a loved one.

Acquisitiveness with discrimination for those who enjoy collecting is splendid, but without it is foolish. Acquisitive people buy things for their own pleasure, to impress others or simply out of habit – they spend for the sake of spending because getting something new gives them pleasure.

Indecision about keeping things because they might have value or be useful some day frustrates organizing efforts. Also, indecisiveness about where things properly belong stalls organizing solutions and results in diminished storage area for necessary belongings.

Lethargy is the easy way out of confronting your disorganization. People who avoid making necessary efforts postpone the inevitable, and must then cope with the inconvenience of clutter, diminished clean area and resulting guilt. People who are lazy about putting things away need a realistic plan. Some individuals may need to overcome psychological stumbling blocks or perhaps recognize they prefer talking to tackling the job.

Overextension is common for enterprising individuals. People who are over-extended may need to reevaluate their priorities or find alternative help to fulfill their organizing needs.

You'll have to decide for yourself which of these categories apply to you. You'll probably find multiple reasons why you're saving things.

For example, you might be sentimental over old letters and cards, an avaricious book collector, indecisive about keeping your children's baby clothes and drawings, lethargic about picking up your clothes, irrational about your ever-expanding yellow plastic butter container collection, and over-extended during the holidays and tax season.

The point is this: You have to recognize and understand *why* you do the things that you do *in each individual case*. Only then can you look at yourself objectively and make logical decisions regarding your options.

SAVING THINGS
AND MAKING CHOICES

- CHAPTER II -

SAVING THINGS AND MAKING CHOICES

The Three Options

Saving things falls into two categories – short-term and long-term. You'll need a special place to keep short-term things temporarily and a permanent storage area and a plan for possible expansion for long-term items.

Giving away or passing things along is an honorable deed. Just set them by the front door in a shopping bag with a sticky label to designate a friend or favorite charity and grab it the next time on your way to the car.

> *I will never forget the wise words of my father-in-law, a kind and generous man to his family, who believed, "It is better to give with a warm hand than a cold one." He valued being able to see the joy he brought reflected upon his children's faces.*
>
> *In spite of my objections, a dear friend insisted upon giving me a small silver Turkish teapot I once admired. "When you give something you treasure to one you cherish, it is with you forever."*

Tossing away or recycling unnecessary and unwanted items is a cleansing experience which can give one a feeling of well-being.

The last two options are the best because you won't have to concern yourself with it ever again.

Making Decisions

Make hard and fast decisions as to whether or not you need to save certain items. Designate specific bookcases, cabinets, drawers or storage areas to house your collections. Perhaps this might entail decisions about:

- Books and magazines
- Children's artwork and papers
- Clothes and shoes
- Fabrics and crafts
- Letters and greeting cards
- Toys and games

Define What is Important for You to Save

The things you value now may not necessarily be important for the person for whom you are saving them. If your children are not as sentimental as you are, they will eventually throw away all those mementos you've been saving all these years. Rather than postpone the inevitable, dispose of these things now or give them to someone else who would appreciate them as you would.

Sentimental Saving

If you have children, you undoubtedly receive an abundance of papers you are required to deal with on a daily basis. If saving their artwork, handwriting samples, special papers and projects is important to you, then store each child's best work in a large gift box for each grade level. At the end of the school year, go through the box and determine which ones you want to save and which ones you want to toss.

I keep four such matching boxes open on a shelf in a closet where I can easily toss papers inside for my four children. I always ask for a large gift box whenever I buy anything at the store that has the handsome silver gift boxes because they are durable as well as attractive.

In higher grades, it is advisable to save all of your child's work until the end of each semester, just in case of a discrepancy in which the teacher's grade book indicates some papers were never turned in.

One year, my daughter had a teacher whose paperwork disorganization resulted in her continual neglect in properly recording her students' papers and grades. Often, she relied on students to input grades into her computer, and the results were less than perfect. Fortunately, we had saved all of my child's school work, so when the teacher claimed that some assignments were missing, we were able to produce the missing papers. This continued to be such a problem that we eventually began to make a copy of each paper and made notations of when and how it had been handed in on the back of it.

Save It for Someone Special

Consider your children, co-workers, friends and even your friends' children when you're cleaning out your closets and cupboards. What may be no longer useful to you may be someone else's treasure.

An acquaintance disposed of a parent's estate one year and regretted it the following year when his son graduated from college and had to set up his first apartment.

I have a few close friends who have given me some wonderful hand-me-downs. They aren't sentimental and have insisted they don't want them back. Because I recognize that I am sentimental, I've packed them away with the thought that it would be a fun thing to give their children when they have their own children. Perhaps their wives would enjoy a few sweet mementos of their husbands' childhood.

I've also saved all of the neighborhood kids' drawings over the years with the same intention. They don't occupy a lot of room and I couldn't bear to part with such precious gifts of the heart.

When my niece was very little she wrote me a sweet little thank you note for a gift I had sent. Years later, she visited me and was flattered to see it framed and hanging on my bedroom wall.

If you aren't using something, then return it. How many times have you bought something, found that you really don't need it and are just too lazy to take it back? It's dysfunctional, takes up space and you're out the money it costs.

I've visited companies where the amount of discarded office supplies and equipment is just astounding. By creating an "orphanage" in supply rooms, so much can be salvaged for someone else's use. If you're not using something, return it to the supply room and avoid cluttering your work space.

Frogs and Chickens

Do you really want to be surrounded by all the things you have accumulated over the years? Are your things there by happenstance?

The back wall of a favorite teacher's classroom is green with frogs – gifts from students over the years. When asked if he liked frogs he glanced at the wall, smiled, and answered, "Wouldn't you think so?" I didn't pursue my questioning, but noted he never answered affirmatively.

The ten baby chicks hatched in my son's first grade class soon needed a home so I built coops with nesting boxes and grain bins on our property. "Chicken Nudel Coop" became well-known and, although the chickens were my son's pets soon I, too, began receiving chicken-related gifts.

White Elephants

How many times have you received an outrageous gift that you don't like, can't use and don't know where to put? The perfect solution to this recurring situation is to make intelligent choices beforehand. Think ahead about what it is you want to start collecting and get the word out tactfully, before you receive another notorious "white elephant". Take size and price also into consideration when you're making your decision.

My miniature perfume bottle collection started by chance one year when my godson gave me a tiny, handsome silver and crystal perfume bottle. I mentioned my delight to a dear friend who gave me another pretty little perfume bottle. My collection started, and now those who know me are aware of my fondness for these handsome little collectibles. In retrospect, I couldn't have imagined a more perfect item to collect. Because of their size, they don't take up much space and can be arranged most attractively. Additionally, they encompass a great price range; attractive, miniature perfume bottles can cost anywhere from $8 on up.

14

Collections

When you group similar things together you can create both an eye-catching focal point and interesting conversation piece. Attractive collections give insight into a person's character.

Some of the collections I have accumulated, whether by choice or happenstance, include clusters of framed photographs on tables, a collection of tins on top of my kitchen cabinets and on shelves over the windows and doorways, antique inkwells and fountain pens on desks, opera glasses and lace gloves on a dresser, copper and tin boxes in display cases and, in the bathroom, tiny perfume bottles in the counter and baskets full of soaps, lotions and bath salts next to the tub.

If you have a conversation piece or something unusual that you truly enjoy, try to build onto it and develop a collection of similar or related items. Learn as much as can on the subject and become an expert. You will be pleased at how gratifying it is to be knowledgeable and to have the ability to speak intelligently of your specific interest. Such ability lends itself to uniqueness and to becoming a person of substance.

I think that it is important for children to develop their own interests. Children love to collect things. Their collections help to make them unique, set them apart from their siblings and enhance their self-esteem. A prize collection enables a child to participate in dinnertime conversations while entertaining guests. This sense of pride is most rewarding and will encourage future endeavors.

Books are good for children to collect for more than one reason. The obvious reason is that reading makes them smart. Secondary reasons include the fact that books don't take up a lot of space, are easy to store, do not have loose parts which tend to get lost, can be saved for future generations and can look attractive if properly organized in a bookcase.

Chapter III

GETTING STARTED

- CHAPTER III -

GETTING STARTED

The Big Picture

You wouldn't think of doing a thousand-piece jigsaw puzzle up-side-down or without benefit of the picture on the cover of the box. You need to refer to the picture to see where the different colored pieces belong. Likewise, you need to see your home's "big picture". You need to designate its many areas before you begin putting its pieces where they belong.

Putting the Puzzle Together

When you begin a jigsaw puzzle, you first separate the colors. The blue sky pieces go at the top, the green grass pieces go at the bottom and the red barn pieces go in the middle. Likewise, when organizing your household, items of like-kind should be grouped together. As you would fit the gathered red pieces together to complete the barn, so should you manipulate related household items within one logical place in your home.

There should be a proper place to put everything in your home. If everything is put in its correct place immediately, you won't have to deal with it again later, and you won't have an accumulation of clutter. Make yourself aware of where you put things. Before your set it down ask yourself, "Where does this belong?" Things shouldn't be left just anywhere. If you are dealing with a number of items that go in various directions in your home, determine which rooms they belong in and, at the very least, start them off in that direction.

We have 23 rooms on 7 different levels within a 6,000 square-foot home. To eliminate constantly running up and down stairs, I leave items on the bottom steps. When an armful of items accumulates, they're taken up all at once. Other family members automatically carry waiting things upstairs. Leaving a large, attractive basket near the bottom step can also be a viable solution. If you get an unexpected guest, it is much easier to deal with one basket than twenty loose items one could easily trip over.

Where Do I Begin?

If you feel totally disorganized and overwhelmed, I encourage you to select one room or area and concentrate on it. Closets, bathrooms and kitchen pantries are usually excellent places to begin because they are small and manageable areas. Once your selected area is in order then it's just a matter of maintaining it

Motivation

It is my hope that after you have finished reading this book the many ideas incorporated herein will motivate you to take charge of your possessions and your life. Once you know *where* things belong, the battle is half won.

Try to find a friend who's equally dissatisfied with his or her disorganization. Discuss what you both want to organize, share your solutions and perhaps even challenge each other.

> *One year, a friend and I found ourselves a few years behind in organizing our photo albums. We challenged each other and agreed that the first one to get caught up would have to take the other person out to lunch. It was incredible how fast we got ourselves organized.*

Try motivating yourself by making yourself promises.

> *I do all of the necessary but unpleasant tasks first and save the ones I prefer doing for last; otherwise, I would never get some things done.*

Set a reasonable time limit for getting control of each area, concentrate on one area at a time and don't get distracted by another area. If something doesn't belong in the area in which you are working, then remove it and place it in the immediate next room in related piles.

Only when you are completely done should you address each pile and take it to its destination. Try to work within blocks of time. Try to start and finish each job within an available time slot, if possible. If not possible, divide long projects at natural breaking points.

Guess Who's Coming to Dinner?

If you are one of those people who say that they would love to entertain in their home but cannot because their home is so messy, then this is what you do to get motived:

Invite someone to dinner!

Yes. This is precisely what you must do. Don't think about it twice. Just do it. You will be amazed to see just how much you can get accomplished in the preceding days of a deadline and you'll probably get a good meal out of it, too!

A little trick you can play on yourself every day is to just imagine that somebody is coming to your home. You will look at your home more critically and begin to notice those little piles of papers and clothes here and there that seem to spring up everywhere.

You might want to try to imagine different people coming to visit you. My favorite is Queen Elizabeth.

Dress for the Occasion

You wouldn't wear your formal evening attire to cook a meal. Sure you could, but you wouldn't be very comfortable doing so. Likewise, be comfortable while you work so you are more relaxed and you won't tire quite as easily.

I feel empowered whenever I am wearing a pair of thick, soft socks, comfortable sneakers, hair up in a pony tail and clothes in which I can easily bend. I feel energized; I can move faster.

Listening to those old rock n' roll hits from the 60's gets me moving in tune with the beat and I'm thirty years younger again. A secondary benefit is keeping fit without having to spend time or money working out.

Reward Yourself

Put yourself on a commission-based salary. Put dollar values on certain tasks you need to perform and pay yourself upon their completion. Use only earned money for your entertainment or treating yourself to a new outfit.

For short-term rewards, promise yourself something particularly enjoyable upon completion of a project.

To really pamper myself after a hard day's work, I find soaking in a hot bubble bath with a book and a cup of tea to be gloriously relaxing. Curling up with ice cream in a glass bowl with a long-handled silver spoon can do the trick, too.

Different Strokes for Different Folks

If you have ever had occasion to be a volunteer, you realize how extremely rewarding it can be. People love you. They pay a lot of attention to you, tell you what a wonderful job you are doing, tell you what a good person you are. Nobody criticizes you. You become the recipient of a lot of positive verbal stroking.

You may work half as hard at home, but do the warm, fuzzy feelings come to you there? Chances are, the answer is no. Let's face it, working by yourself at home is lonely work and efforts are often unrecognized. You may not feel appreciated.

Understand the underlying reasons why you prefer these activities outside of your home. Learn to be a volunteer in your own home and personally reap the rewards of your efforts.

Hearing Voices

There should be some point at which your internal judgment center tells you, "Okay, enough is enough!" Listen to this tiny voice and heed its warning, or else the louder, more obnoxious voices of Guilt and Self-Degradation will begin haunting you mercilessly.

The Lonely Hearts Club Fan

Whether because of a loss of a dear one or fear of being alone, some people have definite needs to be around others. For these people, staying at home any longer than it takes to sleep, shower and dress is a near impossibility.

Start a lonely hearts club, find someone equally disorganized and take turns visiting and organizing each other. Four hands are better than two and you will find that the amount of work that actually gets accomplished is markedly greater than if you worked alone – not to mention how the time will fly by when you are with your friend. More than likely, you will bring laughter and joy back into your homes, be able to look at yourselves more objectively and thereby bring more balance to your lives.

Your Best Friend

Sure, spending time pursuing outside activities and friendships can be pleasurable; however, after the hours have floated by and you are back home again, you are exactly where you were when you left. Control your compulsive socializing urges. Dare to spend more time alone with yourself to get yourself more organized and reap the benefits of your labor.

You are your own best friend. Who likes to go into all of your favorite shops, loves everything you pick out and never has to get home until you do? Who else knows exactly how you're feeling, always agrees with you, never abandons you, is there for you 100% of the time? You! You are your own best friend. Get to know this forgotten person and learn to truly enjoy being alone. Don't depend on others for your happiness. True happiness comes from within.

Don't Drop the Ball

Don't drop the ball on the first yard line and walk away from the game. Keep going and score that touchdown. Always find closure with your undertakings. Don't be satisfied with doing just the minimum amount of work. Try to go that extra yard. Take a second glance around and see if you can improve it and make it better. Anticipate how you will use it and how it can serve your needs better. There might be just one more thing that you could do to produce superior results. Strive for completion and excellence.

Be Kind to Yourself

Make a concerted effort to complete each task, so that you won't have to come back and deal with it at a later date.

Whenever I change clothes, I take the extra few minutes to put everything where it belongs so that the "later me" won't have to pick up after me.

Don't forget that the "later you" is really yourself and will not be too thrilled about doing the pick up work. Be kind to yourself.

Tickled Pink

Take pride in your ability to undertake a task and accomplish your goals. Be aware of how you feel about yourself whenever you get something accomplished. Think how marvelous it is to have an extraordinary internal reward system residing within you. Try to keep these good feelings coming on a regular basis and maintain yourself at that constant elevated level.

There's No Place Like Home

Its not uncommon for people to use their homes as they would hotel rooms and be always on the go. Enjoy your home and learn first to live contentedly. Contentment lies within one's self. Not without.

Model Living

Respect yourself. Your surroundings are a reflection of yourself and define you. Ask yourself how you perceive yourself, then judge your environment. Have you created a milieu at par with your personal expectations? Don't sell yourself short.

Avoid dwelling on dysfunctional areas. Concentrate instead on envisioning that space being ideally used, both in purpose and furniture placement and work toward that goal. Many pictures in decorating magazines are actually homes of real people. Imagine your home as next month's special feature and create your own picture-perfect environment.

Come on in – the Water's Beautiful

Plunging into your disorganized room is like diving into a pool. Although the prospect of diving into cold water is a bit intimidating, once you're in the pool your body quickly acclimates to the water's temperature. Likewise, the looming presence of a messy area in your home might send a chill of resistance through your fragile psyche.

One Saturday afternoon, at 1 p.m., a small, embarrassed family who hired me for a consultation, revealed their messiest room to me. No doubt expecting me to throw up my hands like McCauley Culken, they were stunned when I took a deep breath and calmly said, "Let's do it!"

I gave each family member a job – one person to transport all the paperwork to the dining room table, another to take all the clothes to their appropriate closet, drawer or hamper, one to return all the office, kitchen and bathroom supplies and the last to put the tools, crafts and sports equipment away.

When everyone finished their chores, they each put away their own few, personal items, then together pitched in and straightened up the room. Next, I showed them how to sort the overflowing stacks of paper into major categories – automobile, banking, bills, correspondence, credit cards, education, entertainment, household, insurance, investments, medical, memorabilia, personal, photos, taxes, travel, warranties and instruction booklets.

We worked together for awhile and, when we were half-way done sorting the paperwork, I asked them to check their watches. They were amazed to see it was only 1:15 p.m. – that their greatest of fears wasn't so bad after all!

Just remember, when you survey your sea of disorganization, don't hesitate – take a deep breath, dive right in, enjoy how invigorating the organizing process feels and soon you'll find yourself proceeding swimmingly.

The Controller

To help avoid procrastination, imagine a video game called the "Highway to Success" where the object to playing is to reach your goal as fast as you can. To gain points you must overtake each car in your path. Each time you pass an obstacle you gain points and are empowered, and your extra energy enables you to get to the town of Success faster.

In real life if you promptly do what needs to be done you avoid having to slow down. Each time you accomplish the tasks at hand, you clear your path of obstacles, and can concentrate on advancing toward your goal. With each accomplishment you are energized. These successive positive experiences make you feel empowered to continue onto even greater challenges.

In other words, overcoming procrastination is your "vehicle" to success.

Two Dozen and Three

There's an old Chinese proverb, "If you want change in your life, move twenty-seven things in your house."

Return order in your life. Adopt this ritual and put twenty-seven items in their rightful spots each day. This simple, methodical practice quickly produces results with minimum effort. Just think, as many as 837 things will slip into place each month and 9,855 every year.

Accentuate the Positive

Concentrate on the positive aspects of decluttering your home or office. Avoid the negative, sequential thought process – "I should do it, but I don't want to because it's not fun, so I'll do something that I enjoy more." Instead, tell yourself, "If I finish this project, I'll regain use of my desk, my room will look better and I'll be much happier." Focus on how relieved and proud you'll feel of yourself for completing that long-deferred project and how wonderful it will be to reclaim lost space.

MAGICAL RITUALS

- CHAPTER IV -

MAGICAL RITUALS

Don't Go Out Alone

Make it a habit never to leave a room without making a cursory glance around to see which items need to be transported to other rooms. Even if you are not going to that particular room, you can usually start an item on its way in the right direction. At the very least, you've eliminated the clutter from the first room and given the item its first leg of travel to its destination.

Take advantage of mobile family members.

If I happen to be folding the laundry and notice someone on their way upstairs, I ask them to carry up some clean clothes. If I'm unpacking groceries in the kitchen and someone is about to go upstairs, I'll ask them to take the upstairs bathroom supplies with them. Likewise, anybody on their way outdoors is a prime candidate for carrying out the garbage

Gather Your Thoughts and Plan Your Day

Staying organized requires daily diligence. Take advantage of the time that you are alone to organize your thoughts and better plan the day.

I do my best thinking in the morning while in the shower when my mind is fresh and body relaxed. I use to find myself forgetting my ideas afterward, so now I keep my son's crayon soap handy for jotting down notes on the wall. Later, after transferring my notes, the soap can be wiped off during the clean-up process.

Another beneficial time for me to concentrate is while driving in the car. If I'm alone, I often keep the radio turned off to relax, enjoy the peace and tranquility and let the creative thoughts flow.

Always try to have a pencil and pad available to jot down your ideas in various places in and about your home, office and automobile. Stick them in your pocket if you are going outside to do some gardening or just going for a walk. Keep them near your TV, on your night stand and in the bathroom.

Before going to bed each night, plan the following day. Write down your telephone calling list and numbers, your appointments and errands, as well as the anticipated time on a Daily Planner. (See page 194.) Put related items in your car. Double check for lists, receipts, coupons, colors and measurements to avoid making unnecessary trips. And don't forget to map out your driving strategy in order to save on time, gas and patience.

Functional Work Areas

Identify areas of your home as well as their functions. For example, you may decide that the kitchen counter and clothes drier are not proper homes for the mail, bills and children's school books. A spare bedroom could double as an office and be a more practical place to do homework if a desk and filing cabinet were added. Perhaps there is room in the corner of the kitchen for a desk just for paying bills.

The kitchen and laundry room are two busy areas which must be orderly in order to be functional. You need counter space to prepare meals and counter space to fold and organize clothes. It is, therefore, a priority that these areas remain free of clutter.

I am a strong believer that all family members, both young and old, should have their own desk. Children, starting around the age of seven, should have their own special place to do their homework. Adults require adequate work areas to pay bills, keep records, fill out tax returns, write letters, keep track of their projects and do their filing. Desks in the kitchen are extremely functional and quite likely to get the most use.

Since the arrival of the home computer, many desks have inadequate surface work area. The computer and its related equipment take up a good portion of most desktops, thereby diminishing space to spread out books and papers. Buying a computer desk is a very wise investment. They provide room for the computer, monitor, keyboard, mouse pad, printer, scanner, FAX, telephone, disks, files and more. As a rule of thumb, always buy as large a desk as possible. You'll grow into it eventually.

When our ten-year-old son inherited his older brother's computer, we bought him a six-foot long, five-foot high reproduction oak rolltop computer desk. We mentioned to the saleswoman that it was so big that he could sleep inside of it. After we left the store, she laid down inside, closed the rolltop and got locked inside.

Related Things That Need Homes

Try to group related items together and store in logical as well as convenient locations. Check this list of "family members" and reunite any "orphans" in your home:

•Baby books and children's memorabilia boxes
• Backpacks, lunch boxes, thermoses and water bottles
• Baseballs, bats, mitts and cap
• Beach umbrella, towels and toys, cooler, sun block and glasses
• Bills, checkbook, pen, calculator and stamps
• Board games, puzzles, cards and chips
• Cleaning chemicals, sprays, buckets, towels, sponges and brushes
• Comfortable chair, ottoman, lamp, chenille throw, books and dictionary
• Flashlights, lantern, batteries, candles and matches
• Garden tools, seeds, chemicals, sprays and sprinkler parts
• Gifts, wrapping paper, ribbon, bows, tape, cards and stickers
• Hats, scarves, gloves, mittens, purses, umbrellas and boots
• Iron, ironing board, distilled water, spray starch and hangers
• Kindling wood, logs, newspapers and matches
• Mail (incoming), letter opener, calendar, tickler file, pen and waste basket
• Packing material, tape, twine, scissors, scale, labels and postage
• Photo albums, negatives and picture frames
• Picnic basket, blanket, bug spray, plastic utensils, paper napkins and plates
• Sewing machine, fabric, patterns, notions and mending basket
• Skates, helmets, fanny pack and protective pads
• Ski clothes, hats, scarves, mittens, goggles, Chapstick and sunblock
• Skis, boots, poles, snowboards and sleds
• Shoe polish, rags, brushes and shoelaces
• Stationery, cards, stickers, stamps, address list and dictionary
• Telephone books, telephone-address list, message pad and pencil
• Television, TV Guide, channel changer, video games and video tapes
• Vacuum cleaner, attachments and filters

Using Time Wisely

Every minute of each day is valuable. Be conscious of repetitive actions. Every time you move things from one place to another you are wasting time and energy. By putting time-consuming projects in the right place and taking maximum advantage of your available time you can accomplish wonders.

Whoever said that you can only do one thing at a time was wrong. Whenever possible, try to piggyback your tasks. Pair visual jobs with manual ones. Or perhaps combine manual and communicative responsibilities. Doing two things at once isn't as hard as it sounds. Remember: Always try to save time.

When I'm in a time crunch in the morning I brush my teeth with one hand and wipe off the bathroom counter and mirror or read the newspaper with the the other hand.

I might use two hair dryers simultaneously. While using the more powerful appliance with my left hand I use the hairbrush attachment to brush through my long hair with my right hand.

The Project Basket

I keep a basket handy into which I put little jobs. I include everything that I'll need, such as, if a shirt is missing a button, I put the shirt, a button, thread and scissors in the basket. If I'm balancing my checkbook, I put my checkbook, bank statement, calculator and pencil in the basket.

This basket can go anywhere with me around the house or in the car. This procedure will not only aid you in using your time wisely, it will also help keep your work areas tidy. You won't come across a project setting on a counter and say to yourself, "Oh, yes, I have to get to that soon."

The Repair Basket

I keep another basket in which I put broken toys and various items that need to be repaired. It's much easier for me to do all the glue repairs, or take out and use the glue gun, or do minor woodworking repairs at one time. This is also a good activity for children to get involved in because it teaches them how to fix things. My son, at age fourteen, did almost all of these electronic repairs for our household.

Talking on the Telephone

Never talk on the phone without accomplishing something else at the same time. Let telephone time be synonymous with small task time. Here is one thing that you can do:

Empty the dishwasher.

It's a known phenomenon that whenever a mother puts a telephone receiver in her hand, her children receive a telepathic signal and are mysteriously drawn to their mothers' sides. However, there's an obscure antidote that I use whenever I want to make some phone calls in peace without having children underfoot. I simply start to load or unload the dishwasher and ask if anybody wants to help. It never fails to amaze me how fast I can clear a room that way.

Here are a few other ideas:

- Work on a project
- Fold the laundry.
- Sort the mail.
- Straighten the pantry.
- Reorganize and clean the refrigerator.
- Wipe down the appliances and cabinets.
- Clean the oven.
- Wash the floor.
- Wash the kitchen windows and glass cupboards.

- Set your table.
- Start your next meal.
- Comb the dog
- Or, at the very least, file your nails.

I try to do my telephone calling while I'm either cooking or cleaning up after a meal. These are occasions when I have a definite block of time in which I will be performing routine tasks which require minimum concentration so I can afford to spend time on the telephone and still have enough brain power available to carry on a somewhat intelligent conversation.

When my daughter was young I built a Victorian dollhouse for her on a table near the telephone so I would always have a project to do while talking on the phone.

Watching Television

Televisions are time vampires. You can forfeit a whole evening by merely pressing a few random buttons on your channel changer. Decide the beginning of each week which programs you want to watch and limit your television watching to your selection.

Be aware that watching television is a visual and auditory activity and, as mentioned previously, you might try to pair it with a manual task.

Occasionally, I will use this time to comb the dog or do some knitting because I can work without looking at what I am doing for the most part.

I dislike television commercials almost as much as being subjected to channel surfing during commercials by other family members, so I find these few minutes are a perfect time to get a few little tasks done from the project or repair baskets which might require manual as well as visual alertness.

Time in the Car

How many times have you driven across town for some reason and returned home only to remember that you could have done another errand on the way back and saved yourself a second trip?

You can avoid this common pitfall by keeping a running list of all of the places you need to go and crossing the errands off the list when you finish them. Keep this list with you whenever you go anywhere in the car.

If you have things to take or return then it's advisable to simply get them out of your house and send them along in the right direction by keeping these items in the trunk of your car. Remember to check to make sure that the receipts are in their proper bags, too.

To eliminate the thought process of prioritizing errands and to better visualize the most ideal route, I write them down in geographical order. This also saves time and car expense.

I make similar maps for shopping trips to the grocery store. By grouping the shopping items together by aisle, I can save time. I go down the necessary aisles and avoid aisles which contain items that I don't necessarily need. This helps save money and prevents impulse shopping. Just imagine that your paper is the floor plan for your grocery store and pencil in the shopping items on your map where they appear in your store.

When you are away from home, your car is usually your "home base." It should be as well equipped as possible in order to make it functional.

In addition to maps, facial tissues, comb, brush and a first aid kit in the glove compartment of each automobile, I keep a small cosmetic bag containing toothbrushes, toothpaste, dental floss, nail files, nail clippers, tweezers, pain relievers and anti-acids. I keep small change in the ashtray for parking, phone and vending machines.

I also keep a pad of paper, pens and pencils in the door pocket so that I can jot down my ideas and so that the children can, if time permits, work on their homework in the car if we have errands to run.

Coming Home

As soon as you walk in your front door, make a habit of putting your keys and purse in the same place, whether that place is on a hook or in a drawer. Slip your sunglasses and gloves in a drawer. Purses, keys and glasses are three of the most commonly misplaced items, so give them each their own special home.

> *If you are forever losing your glasses, consider invested in a second pair of reading glasses or even over-the-counter magnifiers to keep in various places around your home – such as by your telephone, desk and bed – to save steps and avoid the ever-continuing search for your glasses.*

Immediately afterward, hang up your hat, coat and, if you take them off, line up your shoes. Toss your credit card receipts and other receipts in a designated drawer or conveniently-located decorative container. If you are carrying any packages, proceed directly to the various rooms in which your packages belong. At the very least, send them in the right direction by leaving them at the foot of stairway or at the entrance of the hall where they can be picked up and continue on their way to their destination the next time someone passes.

Make a mental note to follow through and put everything away as soon as possible, one room at a time, starting with the rooms most visible to visitors.

> *I make a concerted effort to constantly keep the front entryway of our home uncluttered. Since this is the first area seen by visitors, whether expected or unexpected, I try to create a good first impression.*

FURNITURE AND ACCESSORIES AS ORGANIZERS

- CHAPTER V -

FURNITURE AND ACCESSORIES
AS ORGANIZERS

Now that you have made your decision as to what you want to keep, you will need specific places in which to keep everything. Whenever you are considering buying furniture, consider it's storage capabilities as well as its function. Here are some pieces of furniture in which you can keep things:

Armoires

Armoires are handsome as well as functional pieces of furniture that are esthetically attractive in any room. They provide enclosed storage with a maximum use of space, usually within arm's reach. Originally designed as large, portable wardrobe closets to store armor, they have blossomed and opened their doors to reveal attractively decorated interiors. In addition to clothing, they can accommodate linens, dinnerware, a computer workplace or home entertainment equipment. Armoires can attractively feature a variety of functional as well as decorative items. Imagine books interspersed with porcelain potted plants, wooden boxes, framed photographs, candlesticks, a clock, and a bronze sculpture.

In my dressing room outside my bath, I put stacks of fresh towels with silk flowers, baskets of specialty soaps and talcs, an antique doll, old framed photographs, a few special books and a lamp inside a fabric-covered armoire.

I also have an antique oak armoire in my bedroom that I use as supplemental closet storage. I glued four rosettes to hold two closet poles, so I can hang my blouses on the upper pole and slacks on the lower pole. The top of an armoire is the perfect place to display dried flowers. Whenever I receive roses, I salvage the wilted flowers by arranging them in a bouquet, tie a rubber band around them and then suspend them upside down from my laundry room drying rack for about four days until they are dried.

Baskets

Baskets serve a multitude of purposes. Keep a variety of sizes on hand to store your collections, so you can either downgrade to a smaller size or upgrade to a larger one. Unused baskets can be displayed on walls and shelves, suspended from kitchen utensil racks or beams, or hung from a chain with half-opened paper clips in your garage.

I put my children's Legos in one big basket with a handle to make it easier to transport and store. For the Brio train sets, I put the track, bridges and tunnels in one basket and the trains, boats and people in another so that they won't have to dump out the entire contents to get to the smaller pieces.

In my guest bathroom I have baskets containing little soaps and sample bottles of shampoo and lotion. There is another filled with soft terry towels and cloths. Attractive basket collections add interest and warmth to any room and, because several items can be picked up at once, keep maintenance time to a minimum.

Bin Tables

In you have room in your kitchen, an old bin table might be just the thing to help you get organized and to proudly display grandpa's antique sausage press or perhaps put that little TV you've always wanted. Usually, bin tables have regular drawers, bin drawers and built-in cutting boards that provide additional work surface space.

In my kitchen, I have an antique bin table under a window on which I keep an enormous antique copper-and-brass coffee maker, an antique ice shaver, an assortment of unusual antique kitchen-related paraphernalia, and a small TV.

The telephone hangs nearby on the wall. Its built-in cutting board turns the bin table into a great little writing desk or the perfect place to grab a quick bowl of ice cream while watching the news.

In one of the two upper drawers, I keep my personal telephone list, which I occasionally update on the computer, as well as my children's school telephone directories and a supply of pencils. Below this drawer, in the table's divided bin drawer, I keep our large telephone book and recycled paper that has a blank side which is just fine for scratch paper. In the drawer in the other half of the bin table, I store cloth and paper napkins and, in the double bin below, I toss lids to plastic containers.

Bookcases and Bookshelves

Bookcases are highly functional pieces of furniture which add warmth to any room. Avoid buying short bookcases as they tend to fill up and overflow rather quickly, their tops become catch-alls, and the space above them is usually wasted. Floor-to-ceiling bookcases are the best use of space. Position three or four together to give the allusion of a built-in library.

Group books of like-kind together. After that, sort by size. Pull the books forward on the shelf for a cleaner look and one that's easier to read than a staggered arrangement.

When I have a number of books of the same height, I lay them down and stack them one on top of another. Not only is this procedure visually appealing, it also acts as a bookend. Additionally, when the spines' horizontal titles are grouped, it's easier to read them.

Cabinets

Whether your cabinets are built-in or free-standing, you should store large or long items inside deep cabinets and store small items in shallow cabinets. If, however, you must mix small and large things together, then keep the small items in a box or basket in the front of the cabinet shelf. To retrieve something large in the back of a cabinet, it's easier to pull out that single box than it is to reach across a number of little things and knock them all down in the process. If you pretend your cabinets' doors are invisible, you will be more inclined to keep their contents straightened.

I have a cabinet with several deep shelves in our family room in which I keep all of our board games. It allows me to store them two across and four high. They can be easily removed and, because they are not jammed together, the boxes stay in better condition.

If you are building a new home or planning a remodel, take some time to look over your plans to see where you could add built-in cabinets. If it's difficult for you to visualize this, then wait until the rough framing work is in the process. You will be able to walk through your halls and rooms and get a real feel for your home's layout design. Take a close look at dead space beneath stairways, under eaves and between walls. If you think you might want to add a built-in at a later date, then put in a header now to eliminate the need for future sheet rock work.

During a construction phase in our kitchen, we had to eliminate our back door. Instead of sheet-rocking over the doorway, we took advantage of the existing header in the wall and built a shallow cabinet between the studs. In order for it not to appear obvious, we built it about a foot up from the floor. The cabinet's ten shelves hold my spices, an antique spice set, a decorative porcelain condiment set, old tea tins, an antique children's tea set and several rows of old canning jars in which I keep an assortment of pasta, rice and dried beans. The glass French doors let us enjoy this visual delight, and keep the contents clean.

Chests

Flat-top chests make interesting coffee tables that can store old magazines. Some old chests have humped tops and look terrific at the foot of beds; they are perfect for storing those extra pillows and blankets. In a child's room, they can hold a multitude of stuffed toys.

We have an old trunk in which we keep all of our skiing-related clothing and accessories. Experience has taught me to keep it all in one place in order to avoid forgetting something.

I also have a rattan trunk in which I have stored some of my favorite old clothes over the years. Now that my daughter is approaching my size, we have been going through its contents. After she's finished making her selections, then it will be time for the rest to be passed along, with the exception of a few sentimental pieces.

Closets

Consider using closets for purposes other than hanging clothes.

When my first child was born, I wanted a place, other than his nursery, to change him. I wanted a changing area near the kitchen and family room where we spent most of our day. I chose to temporarily remodel a hall closet.

I added a full-size shelf at hip level and cut a two-inch sheet of foam, which I covered with soft white vinyl to make it waterproof. On top of that, I put mattress padding and a soft flannel sheet to make it warm and soft for the baby to lie on while being changed or dressed. I installed several shelves above the changing station to store diapers, wipes, creams, towels, washcloths, hairbrush, comb, clothes and even a few toys for him to hold. From the ceiling, I suspended a baby mobile. A lamp shade softened the lighting and a wind-up toy provided music.

To convert a closet to a curio cabinet first replace the wooden door with a multi-pane French door. A closet with a light already inside is a real plus. You could build a dry bar by removing the door and jam and installing glass shelves on top and a cabinet below. If the closet backs up to a kitchen or a bath, you might be inches away from making that dry bar a wet one.

If you have an over-abundance of file boxes, binders and books, consider adding four or five shelves in a double closet. To determine the minimum number of shelves you need, measure the combined widths of your boxes and the spines of your books and binders, then divide the total linear footage by the width of the closet.

Store larger items on the upper and lower shelves, and reserve the middle shelves for medium and often-used items. If you have a surplus of shelving, keep the waist-high shelves empty and available for current projects. Organize them in horizontal and vertical files. You might even use this area more seriously as a desk, work area, or computer center. The advantage of this clever arrangement is that, when you're finished working, you just close the door.

Our old master bedroom is now my office and computer room. I turned the double-door, walk-in closet into a multi-function workroom. There are shelves on the three remaining walls of varying heights and widths.

The waist-high work surface holds my sewing machines, thread cabinet, sewin:M nd hardware organizers. Underneath are a bank of household and business-related file cabinets, my tool chest and a stool. On the upper shelves, I have fabrics, sewing baskets, surplus office supplies, catalogs, binders, each child's newborn memorabilia box and their current year work box. Boxes from previous years get stored in the attic. A full-sized copy machine occupies the third wall, with a nine-shelf paper organizer overhead.

This room is the nucleus of our house in that it holds many necessary and important papers, tools and pieces of equipment. However, nothing in it is very esthetically attractive, so concealed closet work and storage areas create an efficient, harmonious solution.

Coffee Tables

When considering a coffee table to buy, think beyond the surface and explore the possibilities of contained space.

Our children's television room includes an old pine chest with hammered hardware that's durable enough to sit on; video games and equipment are stored inside, out of sight.

Display Cases

Large or small, if you happen to come across a good display case, consider using it to keep and show off your collections. Display cases keep their contents safe and free of dust. Shopkeepers rarely part with them.

I've built my own display cases to house a few small collections. I used decorative molding and brass hardware to trim them. Instead of using plain glass, I used beveled glass as the finishing touch.

If you aren't a good carpenter, consider having a cabinet maker build one for you. Don't forget to line the bottom with felt so your things won't slide around unnecessarily.

Display Racks

Most larger cities have stores that sell store fixtures and display items. These are usually expensive. So, the next time you go shopping, keep your eyes open. If you see something that would be perfect for your use, ask if they will sell it to you or save it for you when they no longer need or want it.

On more than a few occasions, I've passed stores with discarded wire or plexiglass display racks outside. Upon inquiry, I learned that they were thrilled to give them away so they could avoid paying a dump fee. So they won't forget, I have them tape my name and phone number to the bottom of the unit.

Upon getting these unusual little items home and properly washed, I put them to a variety of uses – from displaying a stuffed toy collection to providing extra shelving within a pantry or closet.

Dressers

Instead of laying your clothes inside the drawers one on top of another, file them. Practice different ways of folding similar items uniformly, then store them on end with the folded portion facing up. The object is to achieve a size nearly equal to the height of the drawer.

When you use the drawer's maximum vertical space, you'll be able to store more items. The most beneficial aspect of this arrangement, however, is the ability to view each drawer's contents at a single glance.

Years ago, I bought a tall, narrow dresser for my first apartment. Over the years, my taste in decorating developed and changed. Rather than get rid of the old dresser, I put it inside my closet and used it for additional storage.

Eventually the chest evolved into an organizer in my son's closet for his Lincoln Logs, Construx, Legos and Ninja Turtle figures. The small drawers are manageable enough for him to remove, enabling him to take his collection to his play area, and replace it within the chest of drawers.

End Tables

Traditional end tables, with a drawer at the top and double doors at the bottom with a couple shelves inside, provide the most flexible, optional storage space.

The drawer can be used to store the television guide and the ever-elusive channel changer. This might also be a sensible place to keep a pad of paper, pencils and that extra pair of glasses. The shelving below provides practical storage for video tapes, video games, magazines and photo albums.

Etagerés

More commonly known as bakers racks, these look terrific just about anywhere. They're attractive, as well as functional. I prefer to decorate them eclectically, that is, with a variety of new, old and often unrelated items.

If you look around each room, you'll discover interesting items that are difficult to store because of their size or shape. Plants are safer on an etageré's open-metal shelves, than on most furniture, because of the ever-present danger of moisture spotting wood. An etageré makes a perfect catch-all for unusual items. Here are some decorating combinations:

Bathrooms:	Towels, a silver tray of perfumes, baskets of fancy soaps, crystal decanters of cotton balls and Q-tips, and a few plants in decorative porcelain pots
Kitchen:	Cookbooks, wine bottles, plants, recipe boxes, old coffee grinders, interesting tins, and old crocks
Living Room:	Books, framed photographs, bronze sculptures, potted plants, a small lamp, and an old globe
Boys Bedrooms:	Stuffed bears, books, model airplane, old skates football, baseball and mitt, and trophies
Girls Bedrooms:	Dolls, books, first ballet shoes, music boxes, hats, stuffed toys, antique photographs, and a lamp

Hall Trees

In years past, no proper home was without a hall tree in its entryway. These handsome sentinels were highly functional pieces of furniture which provided a full-length mirror, hooks for hats, coats, umbrellas and purses and even a seat that opened for storage of shoes and boots.

The oak hall tree in my younger children's bathroom provides several hooks so they can easily hang up their towels, a storage place under the seat for their bath toys and a place to sit to put on their socks and shoes.

Multi-Drawer Organizers

I have an antique oak cabinet from an old hardware store that has about 80 little drawers of varying sizes where I store just about every little odd and end in my household. Each drawer has a brass card holder to identify the drawer's contents. For convenience in locating the items, I arranged the labeled drawers in alphabetical order. To give you an idea of what a piece of furniture like this can hold, here is a modified list:

- Acrylic paints
- Ant traps
- Baby door latches
- Balloons
- Batteries
- Bungy straps
- Crystal lamp parts
- Curtain rod hardware
- Extension cords
- Glue and caulking
- Hammers
- Hooks
- Keys and key chains
- Light bulbs
- Locks
- Magnets
- Maps
- Mat knives
- Mouse traps
- Paint brushes
- Pliers
- Plugs
- Ribbons
- Rubber bands
- Screwdrivers
- Shoelaces
- String and twine
- Tape
- Tape measurers
- Telephone cords and plugs
- Wires
- Wrenches

I use a similar, separate organizer for small hardware with the following divisions:

- Finishing nails
- Nails with heads
- Brass screws
- Flat-head screws:
  - w/slotted heads
  - w/phillips heads
- Round-head screws:
  - w/slotted heads
  - w/phillips heads
- Bolts
- Cup hooks
- Eye screws
- Hinges
- Molly bolts
- Nuts
- Picture hangers
- Thumb tacks
- Washers

Shelves

Shelves provide simple, convenient surface space.

I installed oak shelves with captain's rail above my kitchen windows and doorways to display an old tin collection. Each shelf is supported by two decorative oak corbels which are mounted to the wall. These shelves enable me to group my tins together to provide wonderful splashes of color around the room.

In our son's bedroom, similar shelving travels all around the upper perimeter to provide out-of-the-way display for his many handsome and beloved teddy bears.

In my utility room I have two little oak shelves extending out above my washer and drier, which I decorated with antique irons and other laundry-related equipment and products. One could use similar open shelving to separate clean, folded laundry into individual baskets so that each family member they can transport clean laundry to his or her room and put it away.

When you arrange things on shelves, remember to use the space vertically as well as horizontally. Depth is another consideration. Here is an excellent example:

A client mentioned her need to purchase another bookcase for her growing collection of video movies. By storing them in the traditional on-end book style she wasn't making the best use of the available space. When I turned the videos face-forward and laid them down flat, with their labeled bottoms facing outward, we could stack the videos upward on top of each other. The bookcase could then accommodate several more video movies – to eliminate the need to buy more shelves.

Storage Ottomans

An ottoman that opens provides clever storage. If you're unable to find one to your liking, design and build it yourself. Keep in mind that an ottoman is merely a hinged wooden box that's upholstered and has little legs.

I prefer to keep an extra set of sheets, pillows and blankets in a storage ottoman for emergency overnight visitors. Another good use would be for storing newspapers and magazines.

Chapter VI

Rooms In The Home

- CHAPTER VI -

ROOMS IN THE HOME

The Occasional, Terrible, Utterly-Trashed Room

I hope you will never have to deal with such a desperate situation; however, if you do, know that the hardest part is just getting started. Allow yourself a considerable block of time in which to get the job done. I have found from experience that it takes approximately eight to ten hours per room. Start early and work late. Avoid interruptions. Send children to a friend's, put your telephone on answering, ignore the doorbell and nibble at your lunch while you're working. Don't stop. It is best to start with larger items first and work your way down to the smaller items. Gather and sort these items by like kind.

Large items should be stored on lower shelves, or the floor of a closet, where they can be easily reached and cannot fall off and hurt someone. If you have large items to store that you don't need to access often, then upper shelves would probably be more practical. Try to keep middle shelves available for daily use.

Medium-sized items and collections should be considered next. Hide unattractive items in closets and drawers, then display your more handsome items. To make each room as pleasant as possible, surround yourself with objects, forms and textures that please your eyes.

Finally, sort all of the small items. This part of organizing takes the longest. Remember to sort by kind. It's easier to separate items and put them in piles than it is to deal with one item at a time.

For example, if you dump 350 assorted pieces of hardware in a pile, it's much faster to pick out all the brass items and put them in a pile, then go back and pick out all the bolts and put them in a pile, then pick out all the washers and make a pile, pick out and pile the nuts, then nails. You'll end up with an odd, but manageable, assortment of hardware you can deal with in small groups.

If you have time constraints and an over-abundance of small items, put the entire mess in a big plastic tub, basket, or cardboard box and address this rogue pile at another, more convenient, time. At the very least, your little mess will be reduced to one single location, where it's now contained – a project-in-waiting.

Keep a garbage bag or sack handy, and when it's full put it by your front door. Designate other bags to pass along to friends or donate to organizations, once they're filled, take them to a place near your front door, too. You may want to designate another bag for recycling. When you're ready to make that trip to the garbage or your car to haul your castoffs away, you'll experience inordinate feelings of pride, accomplishment and well-being.

I've visited children's rooms where absolutely everything was dumped on the floor. In cases like this, the first thing I do is make the bed and arrange the decorative pillows. Then I arrange the stuffed animals and dolls. After that, I begin with the larger toys. Usually, by then, most of the clutter has been taken care of and what is left is an array of smaller, unrelated items.

At this point, children can be extremely helpful. They're closer to the ground, so they can pick things up off the floor for you. You can make it a game for them to see how fast they can pick up all their little collections. Because their concentration skills are limited, it's best to do just one category at a time. Challenge them to time races. Children love to win and will want to play again if you're an animated looser.

If they are unenthusiastic about it, you can inspire them by pretending to be just as unenthusiastic by saying something like, "If there are any Hot Wheels you want to save, just put them in this shoe box. We can shovel up the rest of them with all these Legos and give them to Bobby's little brother."

Or, "Don't worry. Any toys you don't pick up, will be sucked up by the vacuum." That works wonders, too!

Changing Use of Rooms

Take a hard look at your home or office environment. Ask yourself whether the original purpose of each space or room reflects its best possible use today.

It's very common for families to maintain unused rooms, such as guest bedrooms and rooms for children who have left the nest. Beware of rooms that have no use other than as shrines of former occupants.

Think through your routine activities and note where you spend your time performing them. Is there a room where you could set up a special place or corner to do any of the following?

- Do computer work
- Make small repairs
- Pay bills
- Play board games or do puzzles
- Prepare taxes or projects
- Read
- Sew and iron
- Study
- Update photo albums
- Work on projects or crafts
- Wrap gifts
- Write letters

I converted one such room to a combination project-reading-sewing room for a client. The chair-and-a-half I selected opened into a sleeper and its matching storage ottoman stored blankets, pillows and sheets. This clever, space-saving arrangement provided a comfortable place to sit as well as a practical solution to the visiting guest dilemma.

The Home Office

With growing numbers of people working out of their homes, the cute little correspondence desk neatly tucked into the corner of the bedroom or living room has grown into a large, handsome multi-purpose computer desk and moved out of the bedroom, down the hall and into a variety of other rooms.

One of my clients, a landscape architect, had a make-shift office in her family room kitchen, and her drafting table in her master bedroom, which was cluttered with business files, books and plans.

Because her master bedroom was the largest room and the most pleasant to be in, with plenty of natural light and a view of her waterfall and Japanese garden through a windowed alcove, it seemed only logical to designate this room as her office, the place where she'd spend most of her time each day.

We relocated her bedroom furniture to one of two cozy bedrooms in the front of the house, where everything fit nicely. The new bedroom window view is less spectacular, however, she normally spends time in the bedroom after dark and, anyway, her eyes are closed when she's asleep there.

The Bedroom

As soon as you get up each morning, make your bed. After you shower and dress, hang up your clothes, put away your shoes, and relegate dirty clothes and towels to the hamper. Take a quick look around the bedroom and bathroom to make sure everything is tidy. Grab that filled waste basket on your way out of the room, along with anything else that needs a lift to the next stop. Now look at your clock. You've been up for only 35 minutes, you're prepared for the day, and you've already straightened one whole room. Congratulations!

Closets

I stored my favorite clothes from the 1960's in an old wicker trunk. My daughter was repeatedly asked by her high school classmates where she got such "rad retro clothes." When she answered, "From my mother's trunk," her admirers would respond, "Where's My Mother's Trunk? Is it a new shop in town?"

When finding room to hang up your clothes in your closet becomes a strain it's time to downsize your wardrobe. Remove and separate clothes that go to the mending basket, the cleaners, the tailor, a relative, a friend, a charity or the rag bin, and get them out of your closet.

When it's time to weed out those old clothes, turn it into a social event with a good friend to get a clean closet and more than a few good laughs. You're more inclined to toss out clothes when someone snickers at you.

Sort your clothes first by kind and then by color. Start on the upper closet poles with short-sleeved blouses and follow with long-sleeved blouses, vests then suits. On lower poles, fold slacks over hangers and hang skirts by graduated length. Hang dresses in another section that begins with short dresses then graduates to longer-length dresses. Hang long garments by the wall to create space in the middle of the closet for a dresser or a cabinet for accessories.

Categorize each section by color. First hang the white garments, then beige, yellow, green, blue, purple, red, pink, brown, black, polka dot, striped, patterned, then plaid. This makes it easier to locate a particular item because you no longer have to scan the entire closet – and it looks so much better than when everything's in a mysterious jumble.

Transparent, zippered organizers that hang from closet poles keep sweaters visible, accessible, clean and moth-free. You can store purses the same way in order to see at a glance what choices are available.

Our bedroom's walk-in closet is long and narrow. It has a closet pole running the length of one wall and a blank wall on the other side. On my husband's side, I mounted racks to the wall to hang his ties, belts and suspenders. On my side, I screwed an eye bolt into the uppermost stud and attached a five-foot brass chain. My skirts hang down from the underside of the chain's alternating links. These 30 skirts which would otherwise require early three feet of my closet pole only use an area 7 feet high by 16 inches wide by 6 inches deep .

Shoe organizers that are suspended from closet poles are more accessible, less likely to get dusty and, because they don't clutter up the floor, it's easier the vacuum the closet floor. Also available are tilt-front, stackable wooden shoe cabinets that hold a dozen pairs of shoes each. If you prefer keeping your shoes in their original boxes, consider removing the small end of the box so that you can easily view and slip out each pair.

Dresser Drawers

Neatly fold all the clothes you put inside your dresser drawers to utilize the allotted space to the maximum. For example, if you fold clothes into thirds rather than in half and turn them sideways you can use up extra drawer space.

I prefer to "file" my sons' t-shirts on end rather than lay them flat in piles. That way they can see all of their shirts at a glance. I place them in juxtaposition with other filed clothes for support. Shorts, sweatshirts and sweaters can be organized in the same fashion. Additionally, I group these clothes together by color for quick retrieval.

Small or unusually shaped clothes such as bras, panties, and bathing suits can be difficult to fold. Because they don't usually wrinkle, consider foregoing the pretense of folding altogether. Just toss them into appropriately sized baskets or boxes and store them up in your closet on a shelf. Either label each box or use clear plastic boxes, so you can easily see the contents. This might be preferable to an unsightly, messy drawer.

Linen Closets

These are relatively easy closets to maintain because most items can be folded, such as blankets, towels, bed linens, tablecloths and linen napkins. Begin with the blankets; store the seldom-used one on the top shelf and the ones you use often on the bottom shelf. Use the middle, more accessible shelves for the items you use often.

I fold and store all my blankets, towels, sheets and pillowcases in such a way that I only see the folded end and not the multi-layered edges. I fold them so that they are all the same size and can be neatly stacked one on top of the other. These two little habits make the closet appear orderly and visually appealing.

If you are under construction and have the opportunity, I suggest that you install an outlet and store a Dustbuster and rechargeable flashlight in the linen closet for practicality and convenience.

The Kitchen

The heart of every home, the kitchen is used more than any other room in the house. It contains innumerable amounts of items, has more things constantly coming in and going out to the garbage than any other room in the home, and hosts numerous meals and snacks – requiring lengthy preparation and clean up each day.

The kitchen is the activity center of every home. It is the room most often used for projects and the most likely recipient of orphaned papers and belongings. Keeping the kitchen organized take diligence and perseverance.

Kitchen Drawers

The drawer nearest to the stove should contain cooking utensils (slotted spoons, ladles, spatulas, etc.). Knife, fork and spoon sets should be in the drawer directly under the china because whenever you need a plate or a bowl you usually need something with which to cut and/or eat it.

The upper drawer nearest the telephone provides premium space for office supplies. I fill this drawer with small pads of paper, pencils, pens, markers, stapler, staples, paper clips, a paper clip remover, a small calculator, rubber bands and a rubber finger for sorting.

> *I save shallow boxes – such as the type your blank checks come in from the bank and sometimes durable, molded plastic inserts from gift boxes – and position them so the entire drawer is tightly divided into multiple deep sections, which molded plastic drawer organizers often don't provide.*

I fill another kitchen drawer with dividers to separate a plethora of items such as can openers, potato peelers, meat timers, corn on the cob holders, straws, skewers, coasters, fancy toothpicks and more.

> *I store groups of seldom-used items, like pastry kits and cookie cutters, in resealable plastic bags in a lower drawer so they're intact and visible.*

In the second drawer down, I "file" all of my dishtowels, potholders and aprons.

I fold my towels over three times to utilize the depth of the drawer, so that all the towels are visible at a glance and none are buried under others. I also keep a box of tissues in there, together with a few face cloths for washing messy little faces that appear in my kitchen.

In the third drawer down, I keep all of my children's favorite unbreakable cups.

Ever since my children were little, I've kept their cups in this special place located between the sink and the refrigerator so they could help themselves without having to climb on top of the kitchen counters.

Another lower drawer holds children's plastic plates. Whenever they help me empty the dishwasher, it gives them something safe and unbreakable to put away. This system has saved me a wealth of time – and enables them to be a little more self reliant.

Consider using drawers to store boxes of plastic wrap, aluminum foil, waxed paper and assorted plastic zip-lock bags. Or attach one of those space-saving units to the back of a door to hold the long, narrow boxes. Either of these solutions will free up space on the shelves of your cupboard.

Once a box of cereal or other dried food is opened and partially consumed, notice how much air it contains. By removing its plastic-bagged contents and discarding the box, you save shelf space. Be sure to clip necessary cooking directions and slip them inside the bag before you secure it with a rubber band or twist tie.

I keep all of my plastic bags of pasta, rice, dried beans, nuts, croutons and popcorn in a shallow drawer, where they fit snugly together and can be easily viewed.

You might designate another drawer to keep all of your boxes of crackers. An alternative method is to keep the crackers of opened boxes in one large, bread-size plastic container. You save space by eliminating the half-empty boxes. Don't discard crackers. Rather, use your older crackers for cracker crumbs.

I have an enormous antique tin cracker box on my counter where I keep all of my crackers. They stay fresh inside, are easily accessible, and the tin adds the perfect decorative touch to my kitchen.

Kitchen Cupboards

A good rule to remember is to store items by kind and use. Make your kitchen work you – not against you.

Make the best use of space. For easy retrieval, store small items in small areas, medium items in medium areas and large items in large areas.

As a consultant, I find that many people make the mistake of storing small items in large cupboards, making it difficult to find things and the cupboards never look organized. They usually find themselves constantly moving things in front in order to get to the things behind. Keep your small items in a basket or box to easily clear the space and access larger items behind them.

The second rule to remember is to constantly downsize. Eliminate half-empty boxes by relocating the remaining contents. It makes very little sense to waste valuable storage space by storing large boxes filled mostly with air.

If I find myself with a giant box of, let's say, dried potatoes containing only a cup and a half of ingredients, I pour the remaining dried potatoes into an appropriately-sized plastic container or reseal-able plastic bag, along with the instructions which I have clipped from the box.

In designating space in your kitchen, start with your stove. The adjacent lower cupboard should store your pots and pans; cooking utensils should be nearby in a drawer or perhaps kept in a crock on the stove top.

Designate a section of your kitchen with a large counter as a baking center. Having your ingredients and utensils in close proximity is a real time and step saver. Keep measuring scoops inside the flour and sugar and perhaps extra measuring spoons inside the baking powder and soda.

Here is a fairly inclusive list for the cupboards above and below the baking area:

Group A	Group B	Group C
Baking powder	Bowls	Baking sheets
Baking soda	Measuring cups	Bundt pans
Flavoring and spices	Measuring spoons	Cake pans
Flour	Mixer	Cookie sheets
Oil	Sifter	Muffin tins
Sugar	Strainers	Pie dishes

A tip-out drawer in front of the sink keeps sponges and scouring brushes at hand so you don't have to bend down to retrieve items from under the sink. Such a drawer in front of your cook top is an optimal place to store spices, so you can season foods you're cooking without crossing the room. To make such a drawer, simply remove the decorative panel, add a bottom, a short back and two curved sides; then install with hinges at the bottom of the drawer front. (See page 196.)

I relocated a couple's place mats from the top kitchen drawer and stored them vertically elsewhere. I then used the shallow drawer to store spices, which occupied two overhead shelves. Rubberized padding prevented them from slipping around and, once alphabetized, they were quickly accessible.

I have wooden boxes built into the insides of all of my cupboard doors so I can easily access all of my smaller items. Although this does impact upon interior space, understand that when the door is closed, that space is used with the boxes' contents. By eliminating all of the smaller items, I find I can use the remaining cupboard space more efficiently with canned and boxed items.

Designate one cupboard to store your plastic containers. Be careful not to get carried away with saving various containers. It's easy to fall into this trap, so you will have to be firm with yourself and learn to recycle.

Last year I treated myself to matching square clear-plastic containers when they were on sale at my grocery store. They're far more space-efficient and more easily stacked than the precarious round ones. The clear plastic enables me to instantly view their contents.

Store your place mats vertically, if possible, or build a shelf a few inches below another shelf in your pantry.

The Pantry

Whether you have a walk-in pantry or just a single cupboard in which you store your food larder, it needs to be stocked in some kind of order for it to be functional. Here is a fairly inclusive list of its contents:

Boxed Goods

Boxed goods should go on one shelf with the narrow labeled side facing out to insure best use of space. If you have more than one, store them two or three deep or turn them facing forward to maximize space. If you have a lot of wasted space above the top of the box, lay them flat and stack them on top of each other. Make sure the labels are right-side-up so you can read their contents.

Group boxed goods together in order of kind. Here are the major groups of food items that generally come in boxes:

- Cereal
- Crackers
- Gelatin
- Mixes

- Noodle mixes
- Potato mixes
- Pudding
- Rice

Canned Goods

Canned goods should also be arranged in similar and logical groupings:

- Fruits
- Vegetables
- Soups and sauces

- Beans and Mexican products
- Tomatoes and Italian products
- Mushrooms, olives, pickles, etc.

When buying canned goods in bulk, stock your pantry shelves by placing the cans in lines from front to back so that only the front can is visible. Stack a related row of cans on top of it and, providing there is adequate room, a third row on top.

Glass-Jar Goods

I have a very small pantry, so I pour oil, vinegar, soy sauce and other glass-jar items into empty yellow squeeze margarine containers and label the narrow side.

I built small wooden boxes 1/4 inch deeper than these containers and mounted them to the inside of my pantry doors. I store their economy-size bottles elsewhere, because I don't want to fill the prime space in my kitchen with products in gallon- or economy-size containers.

Bulk Goods in Crocks

The best way to store potatoes and onions is to keep them in crocks, which provide large, cool containers. If you have adequate room, you can place them in the corner of your pantry.

I keep three antique crocks of various sizes – filled with red potatoes, sweet potatoes, onions, or apples – on the bricks of my kitchen hearth. These pots are decorative as well as practical.

Small Appliances

Group together electrical appliances you use every day, such as the coffee maker, toaster, blender and food processor. Consider their location in regard to their function. A rolltop cupboard door would hide your appliances when they're not in use.

I designed a vertical appliance pantry with pull-out shelves with multiple electrical outlets for toaster, blender, mixer and breadmaker for a client with a minimum of counter space.

Counter Tops

To eliminate a client's migrating crumb issue with his wife, I designed a stepped appliance counter for their new kitchen.

A hole in their counter top above the trash cupboard provides quick and easy disposal of trash.

I've created a convenient "coffee corner" in my kitchen. The coffee maker is close to the sink to save steps. I store cups on the lower cupboard shelf, and filters, grinder, beans and instant coffee on the next shelf above it. I keep tea and cocoa there, too. To save time, I keep a measuring spoon inside the instant coffee along with a bunch of popsickle sticks for stirring.

Because I'm a collector, I've conceded approximately one-third of my counter space to kitchen-related antiques, interspersed with modern conveniences. Many of the decorative items are as useful as they are visually appealing. For example, an old French porcelain pantry set holds flour, sugar, cookies, coffee and tea close at hand. An old crock holds wooden spoons and wire whisks on top of the stove. And a triple antique malted milk machine does more than just look pretty!

The Refrigerator

The refrigerator is one area that's often overlooked during home or office organization. To stay functional, your fridge requires constant upkeep. Food should be stored in logical order, wrapped presentably and accessible. You should not have to dig through shelves and drawers to get what you want to eat.

Use the clever space-saving devices your unit provides, like cheese, vegetable and meat bins. If you don't have an egg rack, keep eggs in the meat bin. If you have a third bin, consider storing your eggs, cheese, sour cream, cottage cheese and yogurt there. Separate condiments from the rest of your food because they're secondary and only get in the way.

I try to keep all the leftovers in clear plastic containers on just two shelves. It cuts down on the time the refrigerator door is open when family members are on a survival mission.

My Refrigerator

The food in my fridge's something to behold
Its blue and its fuzzy and its gathering mold
The eggs smell like sulfur; my pudding has skin
A brown mystery casserole dwells deep within.

My refrigerator holds such wonderful dishes
Like mystery ball soup and evil knishes
My Tupperware keeps many delicacies intact
Like captive creepy crawlers for a midnight snack.

My cheese glows bright green; my meat's a pure white
My guests open the door and shutter with fright
When the door's closed and the grimy light's out
A party begins and my potatoes'll sprout.

I long for the day; I wait for the hour
When my lips touch the carton and the milk isn't sour
I've just got to take time to make everything right
I guess I'll clean out my refrigerator tonight.

The Dishwasher

Load your dishwasher as efficiently as possible. Group items of like-kind together to make unloading easier. It's faster to grab four bowls or plates in a row than to pick them out from here and there.

When I load the dishwasher, I put the utensils in order so that when I take out the spoons, for example, I can grab them all at once and not have to bother sorting them from the knives and forks. I load utensils in the same order that I set the table, so the children will be reminded how a table is supposed to be set whenever they load or unload the dishwasher.

Because I have young children, I fill the bottom rack of my dishwasher with plastic cups and plates, so they can unload the unbreakable items. Believe it or not, this is one chore that little ones find fun to do.

They also enjoy emptying the flatware rack after I remove the sharp knives. You're halfway to heaven if you can teach children to rinse out their plastic cups and load them in the dishwasher, too.

Getting the Job Done

Don't be afraid to solicit help. Getting repetitive and mundane kitchen jobs done quickly will free up time to pursue more pleasant activities.

Small children can help set the table. They can put out place mats, silverware and napkins. Naturally, I don't recommend breakable plates and glasses or sharp knives until they're old enough.

Anyone who's old enough to eat at the table can help take their dishes and utensils to the sink or counter and put away the salt, pepper and condiments at the very least.

The kitchen is the center and most important room of every household and should be clean and in complete order at the end of each day. If you wake up with a messy kitchen, you are already at a definite disadvantage.

Shopping Lists

Keep an on-going list in your kitchen so everyone in your household can immediately add items when they notice a shortage.

Some stores offer shopping check lists that reflect where their products are displayed in their floor plan.

If you save coupons, keep both clipped and the yet-to-be-clipped coupons tucked away with your shopping list. You'll be less likely to forget them when you go shopping. Occasionally go through the stack and weed out expired coupons.

Whenever I use coupons, I put them in an envelope and write the grocery list on the front. Since I shop at a wholesale food outlet once a month and local grocery stores in between, I keep two on-going lists at all times.

I write the items in the order they're displayed in each store. I use this map to plan my route; it saves time, prevents backtracking and deters impulse buying. I keep these lists with my Daily Planner. (See page 194.)

Food Preparation

Do most of the preliminary work as you plan your next meal.

While I plan my dinner, whether in the morning or mid day, I take out the cooking utensils each task requires. This step breaks meal preparation into manageable chunks, so it doesn't seem so overwhelming at 5 p.m. with four children home from school.

For example, if I'm going to have a roast, I take out the roasting pan, meat thermometer, baster, salt, pepper and onions. I often scrub or peel potatoes and immerse them in cold water so they don't turn brown. I peel and save carrots, and take out canned goods, along with the can opener, pans, serving bowls and serving spoons. Packaged mixes can be set out with the necessary paraphernalia, too.

68

I set the table beforehand instead of waiting until the last minute. I turn the glasses over and put the napkins over the plate to keep everything dust-free. An added advantage is that you avoid the hassle of having to ask family members to remove their clutter from the kitchen table at dinner time.

By being better organized, you'll have more time available to think about how you could make the meal a little more special – with perhaps a bouquet of flowers, candles or add a special, creative touch. For example, you might display a decorative birdhouse with greenery around it, or arrange your children's artwork as a centerpiece.

Since dinner is one of the few times during the day when our family gathers together, it's important for me to organize my thoughts about what we need to discuss. Dinner presents an excellent opportunity to read that letter from a favorite aunt, share the day's experiences, discuss the news and make family plans.

If there is something you need to discuss after dinner, put related paperwork under your dinner plate, so it will be there, when you need it.

The Bathroom

Because most homes have more than one bathroom, think about your needs for each one. Try not to distribute their contents at random.

We keep first-aid goods in the bathroom closest to the kitchen and backyard since most emergencies arise from those two areas. The guest bath is furnished with little soaps, shampoos, conditioners, lotions, deodorants, perfumes, towels, toothbrushes – and even extra bathrobes.

An oak bathroom tissue cabinet with hinged door also houses a pencil and small pad of paper. A telephone and intercom hang on the wall.

69

The Medicine Chest

To save yourself time and money, group medicines by kind. This system lets you determine, at a glance, what you have on hand for treatment, so you won't make an unnecessary trip to the store to buy duplicates. Before you begin organizing your medicine chest, check the discard date on your old prescriptions and throw out the ones that have expired.

These categories work well for medicine cabinets:

- Allergy medication
- Antacids
- Cold and flu medication
- Cough drops
- Decongestants
- Eye drops
- Nasal sprays
- Pain relievers
- Prescriptions
- Vitamin supplements

Designate another area for first aid, which includes Ace bandages, antiseptics, adhesive tape, antiseptics, gauze pads – and, of course, Snoopy Band-Aids for those really bad cuts.

When odd-shaped items take up too much space on medicine chest shelves, store them vertically. I use old jelly jars so I can see their contents; however, this might be where you can use those sentimental cracked coffee mugs you can't part with.

These are the three categories I use:

- *Dry Items - thermometers, toothpaste and tubes of cream and toothpaste*

- *Silver Items - nail files and scissors, and tweezers and opened nail clippers which can be hung over the side of the cup*

- *Wet items - razors and toothbrushes*

The Vanity

Clear clutter from bathroom counters. Store handy items in attractive baskets or wooden boxes with lids or in a decorative table-top organizer. These clever clutter cutters make cleaning counters easier.

Higher cabinets are easier on your back, minimize water splashing, and allow extra drawer space. Replace awkward deep cupboards with multiple shallow drawers for cosmetics and toiletries.

Cupboards

Keep spare rolls of toilet paper within reaching distance of the toilet, if possible. In the same cupboard, keep other paper products such as personal feminine products, Q-Tips and cotton balls. Don't store these things under the sink's water pipes, because they'll get soaked if the pipes ever leak.

Wire toilet paper dispensers that hold about six rolls of paper can be mounted inside a wall cabinet to keep your Charmin squeezably soft and dry.

Bathroom Drawers

Divide the space in shallow bathroom drawers with an assortment of cardboard boxes to provide designated areas for:

- Barrettes
- Bobby pins
- Hair clips
- Hair ribbons
- Ponytail rubber bands
- Safety pins
- Scrunchies
- Straight pins

Separate your cosmetics into proper categories for quicker access:

- Body
- Face
- Hair
- Nails

Tip-Outs

By removing the cabinet's decorative panels in front of your sinks and adding a bottom, a short back, two curved sides and securing with two hinges at the bottom of the drawer's face, you can create your own "tip-out" drawer. (See page 196.)

I use tip-outs in my children's bathroom to store their toothbrushes, toothpaste and floss, This eliminates the necessity for them to climb up to reach the medicine chest. Children are more inclined to brush their teeth when everything is easily accessible.

Under the Sink

Most bathrooms have a large cupboard under the sink, which is where you should keep bathroom cleaning supplies, unless you have young children and need to keep these items out of reach. Keep economy-size bottles of shampoo and conditioner down there, too, along with a roll of paper towels on a dispenser screwed to the back of the cupboard door for clean-up purposes.

I installed electrical outlets inside the cabinets under each bathroom sink to house a Dustbuster and rechargeable flashlight. By distributing them in bathrooms throughout the house, they can be easily accessed from nearly every room.

I designed a recessed cabinet set into a client's bathroom counter top to house two hair dryers with their own dedicated electrical outlets.

The Shower

You can buy any number of organizers for inside your shower. A simple, plastic-covered wire rack that hangs from the shower head holds supplies directly in front of you at a convenient level. Its versatility allows you to put various things on its shelves and hang other items from its open wire "fingers." However, the white mesh organizer that hangs from the inside of the shower curtain keeps supplies out of sight.

Janitorial-restaurant-hotel wholesale supply houses offer a variety of items that can provide convenient solutions for your home. In addition, institutional-quality products are usually well-made and easily refillable.

I recently bought a triple-lotion dispenser that I mounted to the wall of my shower with its adhesive backing. I filled the three reservoirs with liquid soap, shampoo and conditioner to eliminate most of the clutter in my shower. The unit also features a shelf for hand soap, a holder for a razor, a mirror and a radio.

The Laundry Room

Keep laundry paraphernalia in the order in which you use them on the shelf above your machines. For convenience and to minimize spillage, start on the side directly above your washing machine. Line up your stain-treating spray, then detergents, additives and bleach. Moving along toward the drier, continue with fabric softener, spray starch, distilled water, the iron, then hangers. Duplicate boxes or bottles should be placed behind the first one.

If they don't do it already, teach your family members to pretreat the stains on their clothes before dropping them into the laundry hamper. Children are surprisingly good at remembering to do this because it involves a spray bottle.

Open shelves and cabinets are both functional means of storage. Decide whether you want your items visible or not. Perhaps a combination of the two will suit your needs.

I had no cabinets above my washer and drier, so I built a 12-inch deep oak shelf directly above the appliances. Because the shelf partially extends out over the appliances, the machines' dials and knobs appear to be recessed. I cut out notches for the electrical and plumbing, but they're not noticeable because I use the shelf to display my antique laundry-related collection.

Many of the displayed items are useful, such as the large, white milk-glass jug I use to store my laundry detergent directly over the washing machine. There's a feather duster, a rusty old bucket of soaps, scrub brushes and a whisk broom, along with a few ribbon-wrapped bundles of old clothes pins.

Antique irons, scrub boards, copper boilers and laundry wringers line other shelves; brooms and laundry baskets hang on the wall. Victorian wallpaper and a miniature lamp also help to make the room appear inviting and cozy.

If your laundry area offers extra space, think seriously about how you can improve your sorting process.

I keep six boxes of varying sizes in a lower cupboard in my laundry room so that everybody in my family can sort his or her own clothes. They are marked as follows:

- *White*
- *Dark slacks and jeans*
- *Light colors*
- *Dark colors*
- *Delicates*
- *Towels*

When the boxes are filled, I simply dump them into the washing machine. Each box's contents are the approximate size of a full load of laundry. I also designate baskets for clothes that need dry cleaning, ironing and mending.

If you ever have the opportunity to design or remodel your home, consider where you locate the laundry room in relation to the kitchen, bath and bedrooms. Since you spend a lot of time in the kitchen it's convenient to have the laundry nearby. If you can change loads while you prepare meals, you'll save time. On the other hand, since most laundry is bed and bath related, if the laundry room is near the bedrooms you'll save steps when you put the clothes and linen away.

If you add a second floor to your home, install a laundry chute in a convenient location.

I have a unit that fits between my washer and dryer to store laundry supplies. Multiple ones could be used to sort clothes and ironing. The added counter space supplements the area for folding clothes.

If your telephone doesn't extend to the laundry room, you might install a line as a time-saving device. Even if you have a portable phone, unless you keep it on your person at all times, you'll have to run and find it before answer it. So, it makes sense to have one permanently installed.

The Garage

Because the garage usually contains a wide variety of goods, it can be extremely difficult to attractively and logically store its contents. Examine the items in your garage and either mentally or physically divide them into major categories. Most garages contain items for:

- Automobile
- Camping
- Decorations
- Gardening
- Painting
- Plumbing
- Pool
- Sports
- Tools

Imagine that you're opening for business and set up your store. Start with your largest category and choose the ideal section of your garage – let's call it a department – to encompass its contents. Now find the best place for the next largest category and, gradually, work your way down in size to the smallest department. After all departments are designated, begin organizing each section, one at a time.

I suggested to a client with a small kitchen who lives in the Santa Cruz Mountains, several miles from town, to use part of her garage as a pantry.

If you buy in bulk from a wholesale grocer, think about how much time and energy you could save by unloading and stockpiling your surplus goods a few steps from your car. Why needlessly clutter your kitchen cupboards? If you bought a case of canned goods, keep a few cans on hand and store the rest. When you run out in the kitchen, you can "shop" in your garage. Keep a shopping list posted in the garage and update it when you start to run low on any items.

I suggested another client with inadequate closet space consider building a closet in their garage for storing coats, jackets, hats, umbrellas, lunch boxes, and purses.

Since these are things you only need as you're heading out the door to the car, why clutter your home with them?

You might store old books, files, clothes, toys, household goods and memorabilia in your garage. Unless these items are in a holding pattern to be sold or given away, resign yourself to accommodating them with long-term storage. Don't use prime space for these ancient treasures. Get them up into the rafters or on the top shelves out of the way. Just make certain in your own mind that the things you store are really worth the inconvenience of keeping them and your forfeiture of valuable space.

Sit down and go through that box of memorabilia, make a real effort to be selective in what you decide to keep, then repack your choices in a smaller box.

Get rid of oddball items. Take snapshots or a video instead.

A client's six-year-old daughter couldn't bear to part with her shoe collection so she took a picture of her child sitting in the middle of a "sunburst" of little shoes so she wouldn't lose the special memory.

Gather those few mementos of your great grandparents and save for posterity. Create and frame a memorabilia box of each ancestor to display and enjoy in your home. Write personal details on the back.

Store your holiday decorations in separate boxes in one area of your garage.

Items that need to be taken out should go directly to your car. These include things like clothes you're giving to a friend, books you want to donate to the library, or perhaps a keepsake you plan to give to a relative.

Storage Space and Shelving

In most cases, garage space is poorly utilized. With the advent of closet companies, more and more space-saving products are available. Keeping abreast of the newest gadgets can be fascinating as well as inspiring. New inventions can often be duplicated by a clever homeowner with minimal skill and investment.

Whenever possible, take advantage of enclosed storage. Floor-to-ceiling enclosed cupboards with adjustable shelving are wonderful if you can afford them. They give any garage a clean, uncluttered, finished look.

A more economical means of storage is to use old cabinets and dressers for holding smaller items. Recruit an old desk to do double duty; you can use its drawers to store tools and its surface for a workbench.

Relegate old file cabinets to the garage to store your past seven years of tax files, correspondence, memorabilia and old school papers. This frees your in-home filing cabinet for current paperwork. If you can find one, a metal filing card cabinet can functionally house tools and hardware.

Old trunks are terrific storage places for sports or camping equipment because they're self-contained units. The various paraphernalia can be safely tossed inside and easily accessed.

We built a storage platform that's a little higher and almost as deep as our cars' hoods in the back of our double garage. This platform is like having a mezzanine in our garage; it creates overhead storage that would otherwise be just dead space.

In order to park each car at its optimal location, we suspended a ping pong ball with string from the ceiling. When the ball taps the car's windshield, we know precisely when the car is in its desired, safe position.

If you build your own storage shelving in your garage, be sure to first consider the sizes of the things you plan to store there. Arrange large, often-used items on the lower shelves and large, seldom-used items on the upper shelves. Center shelves should be of varying sizes to accommodate medium and small items that need to be readily accessible.

Attach two lattice sections to the sides of alternating ceiling rafters to provide a clever rack for storing long PVC, dowels and pipes.

If you have exposed rafters and a high ceiling, consider nailing plywood to the rafters to provide a floor for long-term storage items. Structurally permitting, a pull-down stairway and light will turn your platform into an attic.

I have a clever friend who proclaims her attic is filled to the brim and is equally proud of the fact that she knows exactly where everything is in it. Her secret? She made of map of its entire contents!

Use your ceiling space by building boxes with dividers that fit between the rafters. By hinging one end, the box can be tilted downward for storage. These "suspended bookcases" can hold medium and small items that would otherwise occupy valuable floor space. Hooks secure each unit in its horizontal storage position, out of sight. This solution only works to store light-weight unbreakable items, such as fabrics, costumes, clothes, paper supplies such as paper towels, toilet paper, etc.

In an unfinished garage add blocking between the wall studs to provide shelving for small jars of hardware and other small items.

Storage Boxes

If you need to box your goods, consider using same-size boxes, such as bankers boxes, which enable you to stack items tighter. Build your shelves from floor to ceiling and be sure to use each shelf's depth and vertical space. Avoid storing paper and boxed goods on the floor, because the dampness may affect them.

A lovely retired couple who were clients of mine had an entire room that was filled to the brim and overflowing. Every surface was covered; every conceivable space was filled.

They used the room as an office, a sewing area and he built models. They collected various hobby magazines, books, extensive photograph albums, collections and files. You had to slowly walk sideways through the aisles in order to not disturb the staggering eye-level piles.

The room's contents were a culmination of two lifetimes of interests. The two enjoyed spending time together in the room working on their various projects and hobbies and were, therefore, unwilling to part with any portion of it.

I suggested building enclosed floor-to-ceiling shelving just outside the room in the carport breezeway. Shelves were spaced 11 inches apart and 16 inches deep, to accommodate standard banker's boxes, and spanned nearly the entire length of the carport. The completed 8-foot high by 12-foot long cupboard could accommodate 96 boxes!

Related items or items of like kind were grouped and boxed. We labeled each box according to its category and contents, such as:

OFFICE	*PHOTOGRAPHS*	*SEWING*
Taxes	*Family*	*Patterns*
1999	*1945 - 1949*	*Children's*
OFFICE	*RECORDS*	*TRAINS*
Taxes	*Rock n' Roll*	*Lionel*
1998	*1960 's*	*Joshua's*

The labeled boxes were alphabetically filed within their designated area. Now each person uses one section and is responsible for maintaining it. Since the room is cleared of unsightly clutter and the couple can easily access their things, they're both more apt to pursue their interests.

Use appropriately sized boxes to store your goods. Avoid storing air by using a box that's too large. Fill boxes with items of like kind and place heavier objects on the bottom. Be sure to properly label your boxes.

When dealing with multiple storage boxes, arrange them so each labeled box is visible and easily identifiable. I discourage burying boxes by storing boxes two or three deep unless their contents are of like kind, such as holiday decorations. The box in front should contain items that are similar to the ones stored behind it.

Because computer companies recommend retention of the original packing materials for moving purposes and for return of equipment for repair, storage of these ungainly boxes becomes a necessary evil. I suggest storing all such boxes in one place. Whenever possible, store smaller boxes inside of larger ones, but be sure you list the contents of nested boxes, and keep the list where you'll find it.

Bicycle shops sell racks and hooks for bicycles so they can be hung on the walls or suspended from the ceiling. Balls can be stored in sacks and hung on hooks. Skis can be paired up and hung as a unit between spaced, cushioned pegs under their tips and ski poles can be draped over them. Keep the floor free from clutter; hang up golf clubs, tennis rackets, baby strollers, playpens and wagons in addition to the lawn mower, fertilizer spreader, and all those garden and carpentry tools.

Small glass jars are perfect for storing nails, screws and other small hardware.

My father saved my baby food jars to store his nails, screws and other assorted hardware. He made permanent homes for them by screwing their lids to the underside of shallow shelving. To access their contents, he merely had to unscrew the jar. Because they were fixed in place, they never fell or were knocked off their shelves; because they were suspended under the shelves, nothing had to be moved in order to dust each shelf.

I Don't Want
To Want It Anymore

- CHAPTER VII -

I DON'T WANT TO WANT IT ANYMORE

*I need to get rid of this stuff. I know somebody could use it, but who?
Here are some suggestions regarding unloading your various debris:*

Once a Week – Whether You Need It or Not

In our neighborhood, once a week, on Thursday morning, without fail, a big noisy, white truck comes rattling down our streets and stops at each house. A nice man gets out of the truck, empties our garbage into the back of the truck, takes it away, and doesn't bring it back! This is good.

Take advantage of this marvelous service. Take a look around different areas of your home each week and eliminate some of the fluff.

When my file cabinet starts to bulge, I know its time to weed out unnecessary papers and obsolete catalogs from my files.

Recycling

If you have enough room in your broom closet or an attached garage to store the necessary separate recycling containers, you are very fortunate. But, for those of us who have limited space or detached garages, I suggest keeping at least one box as close to the kitchen as possible in which to store all of your cans, bottles and plastics. Before your garbage pick-up, take the box outside and separate it into the correct receptacles.

In our neighborhood, each house have been given three large, plastic bins. Assorted papers go in the yellow bin, glass and plastic go in the green bin and cans go in the blue bin, which makes recycling simple. Convenient push carts with three sets of hooks that hold the three bins vertically can be purchased to save storage space in the garage and save time in transporting the bins to the curb each week.

You can buy both manual and electric can crunchers that can be mounted to the wall directly above your aluminum can recycle box. Some can accommodate multiple cans. By decreasing the size of cans, you save valuable space and reduce the number of trips to the recycle location.

In helping to design a new home, I located a can cruncher inside a pantry. Once crushed, the cans fall down a chute to the garage below where they land in a large recycling bin.

Space permitting, similar chutes for plastic and paper can be utilized. For obvious reasons, it is not advisable to use such a chute for glass products.

If you get daily newspapers, keep them in an attractive basket, crock, or box to eliminate the clutter of newspapers all around the house. At the end of the week they can be easily gathered and packed into a paper shopping bag for recycling.

My grocery store has a recycle bin in front for plastic bags and plastic wrap. On shopping days, I flatten my filled bag and knot it to get out the excess air so they take up less room.

Paper bags are usually well received at your grocery store. Some stores will pay about five cents per bag whenever you shop there and fill them. Also, kindergarten teachers usually love receiving large paper bags for sending children's artwork home.

Did You Know That

According to Green Leaf, a paper recycling company:

- Every ton of recycled waste paper saves 17 trees.
- One ton of recycled paper saves enough energy to run an average home for six months.
- Paper takes up 40% of our landfills.
- U.S. landfills are closing at a rate of about one per day.
- One ton of recycled paper saves 7,000 gallons of water.

Goodyear Blimps

Goodyear blimps are large receptacles of air. You wouldn't want one in your home. Like Goodyear blimps, empty boxes store nothing but air.

I can't begin to tell you how many times I've finished organizing projects that resulted in a staggering amount of empty boxes afterward. This phenomenon is universal and transcends cultural barriers.

People often use the wrong size boxes to store their goods. If a box is too large, you forfeit valuable shelf space to store excessive air. If a box is too small, people lose the ability to close the box and are often unable to neatly stack other boxes or things on top – wasting the space above.

To eliminate the clutter of several small boxes or containers of related items and to simplify the retrieval process, combine similar items and store them in a single, appropriately-sized, labeled box. Try to avoid the Kachinka doll system of storing a box within a box, within a box, within a box. The unveiling of a box's contents shouldn't be a lengthy, frustrating chore.

Sometimes people accumulate excessive amounts of empty boxes in anticipation of future uses. If you must store a supply of boxes, whenever possible, flatten the boxes to save valuable space – when you are ready to use them, you can retape the boxes' bottoms.

Good Junk You Hate to Part With

What to do? What to do? Here's the answer: *Pass It On!*

Having children who've gone through the system from preschool on up, I have found that the teachers of the younger grades are thrilled to receive so many things that would otherwise get tossed in the garbage. Here are a few things that I've passed along to preschools, kindergartens and day care centers:

- • Art Supplies:
  aprons
  brushes
  crayons

magazines with lots of pictures
markers
paints
paper
used greeting cards with pictures
wrapping paper

- Sewing Supplies:
    buttons
    fabric scraps
    ribbons
    thread
    yarn
- Containers:
    baskets
    plastic containers
    tins

- Old Toys and Records

- Kitchen Utensils (for play kitchen as well as sandbox)

- Broken Equipment: (fascinating to take apart and examine)
    adding machines
    cameras
    kitchen appliances
    typewriters
    VCRs

Garage Sales

Garage sales not only help eliminate clutter, they create space and can be monetarily profitable.

When preparing for your garage sale, make sure you have not forgotten anything by going through your house, room by room. Open every closet and drawer. Separate your wares by kind as you begin filling your garage with merchandise, to save time in setting up the morning of the sale.

Before you open for business, make sure you have price stickers on everything you want to sell. Quite often, a neighbor will stop by and want to know what you're asking. Without an established price, you might feel compelled to ask a lower price than what you feel you might otherwise get.

Don't forget to advertise. Whether you put up multiple signs in the neighborhood or invest in an ad in the local newspaper, your sales will depend on the interest you create.

Be realistic. Don't expect to get the price an item might sell for in a shop. Price things to move quickly. Remember, your goal is to empty your garage to create space.

> *Before you even decide to go into the garage sale business, check with your accountant to see if you could benefit more by donating your things and taking a tax deduction than by selling them.*

Compulsive and Impulsive Buying

Let's face it. Shopping can be psychologically uplifting. Understand that a big part of the purchasing process is experiencing this delight. Living in an area with an over-abundance of tempting shopping sources can also make it extremely easy for one to slip into excessive buying. To avoid this common pitfall, make a shopping list and buy only what is on the list.

Be aware of your spending habits. Do you buy things just for the sake of buying? Or, do you buy things on whims? Whether you are a compulsive or impulsive shopper, or perhaps even a clothes horse, pull in the reins and gain control of your runaway spending habits.

Duplicate Buying

How many times have you bought something, only to discover later that you already had one? Or perhaps you bought a second one because you couldn't find the one you already owned?

The problem with having so many things of the same kind is that, after awhile, you can't remember what you have. You may have stopped using them and they slip to the back of the closet or cupboard and take up valuable storage space. When you reach that point, it's time to downsize and reevaluate the best use for that particular area. You'll be less inclined to duplicate if you are organized and aware of what you already own.

Make a commitment not to buy anything until you have used up what you already have on hand.

I suggested to one such client who had a room full of wrapping paper supplies that she temporarily offer a gift wrapping service.

I advised another client who had enough food to fill a bomb shelter that she would be put on house arrest if she was ever spotted near the canned food aisle of the Safeway grocery store.

A third client who had more shoes than Imelda Marcos, had to be warned that the shoe police had been alerted and suggested she avoid all shoe stores in the future.

Put Your House on a Diet

Burn off your house's excess fat. Combine its duplicate contents, rid it of excess containers, and use up what you have before you buy more.

When my nail polish inventory dwindles to a supply of several nearly empty bottles, my creative side takes over and I combine some of the polishes and, quite often, come up with a bottle or two of an interesting color.

This same method can be used for combining white-out correction fluid, glue, shampoo, conditioner, laundry soap, liquid soap, dish soap, hand lotion and body lotion. When combining paints, be careful to separate your acrylic and latex paints and be watchful of the flat, semi-gloss and high-gloss finishes. Never, never combine chemicals or cleaning products!

To downsize your larder, use up what you already have before you buy more.

When my children were little, they enjoyed "Nudelman mystery noodles" which were imaginative combinations of pasta made from the remnants of various packages. Because of the differences in cooking time, I put the pasta requiring the longest cooking time in the pot of boiling water first and gradually added those requiring less.

Other foods that can be combined are jelly, jams, mustard, barbecue sauce or cooking oils.

In spite of having full boxes of cereal, my children often make their own creative concoctions of their favorite cereals.

Also be aware that excessive hoarding of bubble wrap and packing "popcorn" can contribute to the clogging of vital arteries in an otherwise healthy household.

YOU AS YOUR OWN PERSONAL SECRETARY

You're Hired

With logic and consistency, you can be your own personal secretary and keep yourself on track by implementing some basic organizational methods without purchasing an expensive electronic personal organizer or data base software.

The Telephone-Address List

There are four basic categories for most telephone-address lists:

Family   Friends   Resources   Work Related

I discarded our old telephone-address books after I typed their contents on our computer in simple word processing. This computerized listing enables me to easily access and up-date information. When inevitable changes occur, I pencil them in and, when the list begins to appear a bit shabby, I modify the original on the computer and run off copies of the new listing.

Alphabetical lists can be printed horizontally, vertically or in clusters. Below are examples of horizontal and clustered lists in 13-point Helvetica:

(313) 527-0164 Gottlieb, Joshua & Jessica, 14410 Troester Ave., Detroit, MI 48205
(718) 822-6910 Stoller, Adam, 1150 Pelham Parkway South, New York, NY 10062

or

Gottlieb, Joshua & Jessica (Gus & Matt)   *Stoller, Adam (Joe & Rebecca)*
14410 Troester Avenue   *1150 Pelham Parkway South*
Detroit, MI   48205   *New York, NY   10062*
(313) 527-0164   *(718) 822-6910*

Space permitting, it's wise to include children's names in parentheses to refresh your memory on personal correspondence. This might be a good place to jot down birthdays also. How special you would make your friends feel if you remembered their children's names and ages. For multiple mailings, use a label-making computer program.

Resource lists usually include only names and telephone numbers under main categories, such as:

- *Auto repair*
- *Babysitters*
- *Carpenters*
- *Computer repair*
- *Doctors*
- *Electricians*

- *Gardeners*
- *Glass repair*
- *Hair stylists*
- *Housekeepers*
- *Lawyers*
- *Painters*

- *Plumbers*
- *Roofers*
- *Travel agents*
- *Upholsterers*
- *Wallpaper hangers*
- *Window cleaners*

The Special Occasion Calendar

This is a sequential list which records all birthdays, anniversaries and special personal dates in order by month. It is an easy-reference guide. New entries can be penciled in and old entries can be crossed off, but you will probably find that you won't have to retype this list very often.

I have my special occasion calender on my computer where I can easily update it without totally retyping it. Next to each birthday and anniversary, I make a notation as to the year they were born or married so that I won't forget landmark occasions.

Stationery and Greeting Cards

Many people logically store their stationery and greeting cards in their writing desk. By keeping your address book, stamps and stickers in the same location, you create an inclusive work station.

Also, you might want to keep a supply of cards on hand at all times in order to avoid running out to buy a card each time an occasion arises. Try to do all your card buying just a few times a year.

Whenever I like a card enough to buy it, I usually buy more than one. I try to think of who else it would be appropriate to send to and, when I get home, I put a rubber band around it with a sticky label indicating the person I sent it to so that I don't mistakenly send the card to the same person the next year. I do the same for stationery.

If you really want to be organized, take time to check your special occasion calendar and make a list of the people for whom you need to buy a card. Put this list in your wallet, so the next time you're in a card shop, you can make all the necessary purchases at one time.

Personally, I object to paying $3 to $5 for a card that usually gets tossed in the garbage the very next day. I disdain industries that thrive on guilt. Years ago, there was no such thing as Secretaries' Day and Grandparents' Day. Mothers' Day would be more meaningful if children and husbands would choose their own Sunday to honor and celebrate their mothers and wives rather than allow the card industry to dictate to them.

I know a professional woman who shares my feelings. She makes her own cards by cutting out cartoons and pictures and, to me, the fact that she goes to such lengths to convey her good wishes in such a clever and thoughtful way is far more meaningful than spending $3.50 on a piece of paper.

Whenever I send humorous cards that I know my friends will truly enjoy, I don't sign my name. Rather, I take a decorative sticky note, write a message on it and sign the sticky note. In essence, the card becomes part of their present, a chuckle they can enjoy and pass along to another friend.

Gifts

Buy in advance, if possible, to avoid rushed shopping trips and impulse buying.

Whenever I come across something special, I think about who else would enjoy it, then buy in multiples and store in my "gift closet." I always jot the names down on a sticky note so I won't forget or inadvertently send duplicates.

95

No longer do I forget to give a gift I bought and stashed away in my closet. To remind myself, I write a note that details what I bought and where it is, then put it in either my monthly or daily tickler file. If I have already chosen a card, it might also be there.

Wrapping Paper

There are clever wrapping paper organizers available.

The one I prefer can be hung from either a hook or closet pole for storage or folded in half to stand up on a table top for easy access. It features clear plastic velcro pockets for storing wrapping paper, cards, ribbon, bows, tissue paper, gift bags, scissors, and tape. This particular organizer is by far the best because it stores your wrapping paper paraphernalia vertically – to free up shelf and floor space that would otherwise be utilized for its storage. To save more space, I discard the cardboard tubes, tightly roll the papers and secure them with small, soft rubber bands.

Another way of storing giftwrap is to suspend the rolls horizontally on a series of closet poles in a shallow cupboard.

In designing new homes, I try to incorporate a gift closet or gift wrapping area.

Paperwork Limbo Syndrome

You are not in heaven by any means if you are guilty of keeping various assorted piles of paper hither and yon all around your home or office. You are currently existing in "Paperwork Limbo."

To achieve a more utopian level, put your faith in a sturdy file cabinet, a four-shelf, stackable plastic, metal or wooden organizer, and an ample waste basket. With faith in yourself, you will soon become a believer and your life will be heavenly.

FILING
SYSTEMS

- CHAPTER IX -

FILING SYSTEMS

The File Cabinet

Ideally, you should be able to access your most commonly used files from your desk chair without having to constantly get up and walk across the room. An in-desk file cabinet is most recommended; however, a strategically placed two-drawer file cabinet or the bottom two drawers of a four-drawer file cabinet could also be reached without rising out of your chair.

In my office, I have a double-doored, walk-in closet with a bank of two-drawer file cabinets with a wood shelf on top. The wood shelf gives it a finished look and acts as a work surface for my many projects. Overhead is recessed shelving which accommodates a variety of supplies and equipment.

File Storage

Unclutter your files by removing unnecessary paperwork. Have a separate bankers box for each year and store that year's tax return and tax-related receipts inside along with any other important paperwork that is current-year related.

As a general rule of thumb, most people occasionally need to access the past two years' taxes. Anything longer than that should be relegated to long-term, deep storage for at least seven years.

Keep files you refer to daily within arm's reach of your desk, if possible, and never use prime space for dead or old file storage.

Elephants in Your Zoo

You wouldn't build the pachyderm house in your zoo before you counted your elephants. Likewise, when setting up your files, you should initially determine the size of each file before you choose, label and arrange its file folder.

To customize your filing system to your specific needs, first designate the major categories and sub-categories of your cabinet's contents. Next, sort your papers into these multiple groups.

Beware of folders whose contents are too large. These bulging files tend to be unruly when handled and can cause paper retrieval to be a lengthy and frustrating process. Downsize them by examining their contents, dividing them by their obvious differences and identifying them with specific labels.

For example, if you have an over-flowing file of twenty maps and, of those twenty maps, you have one map each of Boston, Canada, Connecticut, Copenhagen, Florida, London, Los Angeles, Manhattan Island, Michigan, New Hampshire, New York, Newport Beach, Sacramento, San Diego, Santa Cruz, San Francisco, Syracuse, Tel Aviv, Vermont, Arizona. By studying their locations, your might decide to group them into the following reasonably-sized categories:

- *California - Northern*
- *California - Southern*
- *Foreign*

- *New England States*
- *New York*
- *Other States*

After your files are in logical order and a manageable size, select appropriate hanging file folders – standard or legal, regular or wide-bottom, plain or color – and then choose the cut of the manila folders – 1/3 cut or 1/5 cut – to contain the papers and to visually duplicate and express your logical thought process.

A functional filing system is one that constantly evolves – growing larger when new files are created and smaller when waste is eliminated. So, by first determining the size of the creature, you'll be able to provide tailored housing for it and retrieve your white elephants more quickly.

Setting Up Your File Cabinet

When you're setting up your files, determine your major categories and file by need rather than by name. In each case, ask yourself, "Do I need this?" If not, then toss it or send it along to the person who might need it. If you do need to keep it, then ask yourself, "Where does this logically belong? When will I need to retrieve it? What will I be needing it for next?"

For example, if you need to gather income figures for annual reports or tax purposes, label your hanging folder "Income" and label the enclosed manila folders with the applicable property or account names.

By doing so, you eliminate the middle step of having to retrieve various account files at the end of the year as well as the double thought process. You won't have to say, "Let me see. Which accounts do I have to pull to compile this information? What did I do last year?" Mistakes and oversights can, likewise, be minimized or even totally prevented.

Be logical. Prepare an alphabetical list of all of your projects. Use hanging files for these major categories and secure their file labels to the extreme left and front of each folder. By positioning the tabs in this manner, they can be more easily scanned. In other words, because the tabs line up in one neat column, the eye will move in one straight line, as opposed to zigzagging back and forth across the width of the file cabinet.

For the sub categories, depending on size, use hanging files or file folders within them with their labels positioned in the second place, then third place, and continue in this fashion by utilizing the three or five possible tab positions, if necessary. For bulky files use expandable folders or wide-bottomed hanging folders.

Techniques such as varied use of capitals and lower case letters can help highlight major and minor categories. For better visibility use a Avery #5366 white file folders labels. Colored hanging or file folders can also flag special files.

Logical filing systems evolve from simple outlines. Model systems should be easily understandable to others. Here is a random example:

A. AMERICAN MARKET
  1. Eastern States
      a. Illinois
      b. Massachusetts
      c. Michigan
      d. New York
          1. New York City
          2. Syracuse

2. Western States
    a. California
        1. Northern California
            a. Sacramento
            b. San Francisco
        2. Southern California
            a. Los Angeles
            b. San Diego
    b. Oregon
    c. Washington
B. FOREIGN MARKET
    1. Australia
    2. Canada
    3. Great Britain
    4. New Zealand

Basic Household Filing System

In an office, file cabinets are necessary for organization and storage of paperwork; however, nearly every household eventually accumulates a wealth of paperwork and a four-drawer file cabinet is usually all that is necessary to bring logic and order to end the madness of paperwork disorganization.

Here is a good basic outline for any household. The words in bold are the labels for the hanging files and the words listed below are the labels for the manila folders to store the paperwork within the hanging files. Once your files are established, it's a good habit to always file the newest paper in front so that, when you have to refer to the previous page, it's always on top.

AUTOMOBILE
DMV - *forms, manual and tests (See Taxes for auto registration fee.)*
Car Make

Label by car model, color or year if you have two or more cars of the same make.

By using the Vehicle Service Record cover sheet (See page 195.) to reflect mileage, improvements and costs, you'll simplify the work you have to do to compute yearly tax deductions.

BABY BOOKS

If the purpose of this metal cabinet is to keep your valuable papers in one safe area, then this might be something that you'll want to include here or under Personal Documents. (See page 109.)

Years ago, the wild mountain fires came up to the ridge behind our home. A friend who was helping us pack whatever possessions we could, reminded me to pack our children's baby books. Fortunately, the fires were eventually contained and extinguished, but many times I have relived that terrifying day and rethought my priorities.

On occasion, I add a few lines in these treasured books to keep them current and, in the process, will inevitably page through them with my four children. Of all the times I spend with my children, these are one of the most joyous. The delight children experience in hearing about themselves as babies is pure and exhilarating.

BANKING

Label by bank name and type of account.

BILLS PAID

Automobile Insurance	**Medical Insurance**
Cable TV	**Mortgage**
Car Payment	**Newspaper**
Credit Cards	**Personal Loans**
Dental Insurance	**Pool Service**
Garbage	**Student Loans**
Gardener	**Telephone**
Homeowners Insurance	**Tuition**
Internet Provider	**Utilities**
Life Insurance	**Vision Insurance**

Label by the name of the company which is usually the addressee on your check, to avoid the double thought process of identifying the service when filing. Be discriminating. Toss out bills that you won't need for future reference or tax purposes, such as your garbage, television and water bills.

Upon coming home, I immediately put my Mastercard and VISA receipts into two separate little boxes. When I get the monthly statement, I verify the entries by matching them to my original receipts, which are already in sequential order, then I staple the corresponding receipts to the back of each page of the bill.

CAREER
Articles
Benefits
Continuing Education
Credentials

Employment Prospects
Evaluations
Letters of Recommendation
Resumes

EDUCATION
Awards and Certificates
Diplomas

Report Cards
Transcripts

ENTERTAINMENT
Clubs
Concerts
Magazine Subscriptions

Restaurant Menus
Sports
Theater

This is where you can keep literature, newsletters, schedules, and programs you collect and even menus you keep for take-out service. For schedules you need to refer to daily, use the Ready Reference Board system. (See page 115.)

GREETING CARDS

Anniversary	**Engagement**	**Rosh Hashana**
Baby (newborn)	**Fathers Day**	**Stationery**
Baby Shower	**Get Well**	**Stickers**
Birthday (child)	**Gift Enclosure**	**Sympathy**
Birthday (humorous)	**Graduation**	**Thank You**
Birthday (serious)	**Halloween**	**Thanksgiving**
Blank	**Hanukkah**	**Thinking of You**
Christmas	**Invitations**	**Valentines Day**
Dear Friend	**Mothers Day**	**Wedding**
Easter	**Newborn Baby**	**Xtra Envelopes**

Many people store an assortment of greeting cards in a desk drawer then shuffle through them whenever they need to choose one. To eliminate this redundant ritual of selection, categorize the cards and file them. Unless the card is unusually large, you can normally store them side by side inside manila folders.

Included in some of my manila folders you might find stickers which pertain to a particular occasion to use as decorations on their related envelopes so I don't forget to use them.

HEALTH INTERESTS

Beauty   **Exercise**
Diet   **Holistic/Vitamins**
Elective Surgery   **Mental Health**

This is where you might keep other personal health interest files, such as Alzheimers, diabetes, heart disease and weight management.

HEALTH RECORDS

Bills - Paid   **Immunization Records**
Bills - Pending   **Test Results**

I have folders for each family member's medical bills. When the insurance company sends the explanation of benefits page, I staple it to the front of the doctor's statement and invoice after I pay it. Next, I record the total amount paid on a summary cover sheet which is paperclipped to the top of the year's bills. When loose papers come in, I immediately file them in their proper folder and have the option of working on them at a later date.

Using this method, I know I've paid a bill by the presence of the staple and, likewise, I know I've recorded the amount paid by the presence of the paper clip. At each year's end, instead of hunting through my files for information, I merely have to total each page for tax purposes.

HOME DOCUMENTS

Appraisals	**Permits**
Assessment Cards	**Purchase Papers**
Comparable Sales	**Refinance Papers**
Mortgage	**Surveys**

HOME IMPROVEMENTS, MAINTENANCE AND REPAIRS

Alarm	**Landscaping**
Carpeting, Flooring and Tile	**Masonry**
Carpentry	**Painting**
Cleaning	**Plumbing**
Decorating and Remodeling	**Pool and Spa**
Electrical	**Roofing**
Fabric	**Telephone**
Furniture	**Wallpaper**
Heat and Air Conditioning	**Window Coverings**

I keep magazine clippings, product brochures and contractors business cards here when I'm considering a new project.

This file allows me to instantly access names, phone numbers and information on previously done projects and repairs. I know who did what, when, why, and for how much. Keeping this file up-dated provides an accurate history of our home.

For carpeting, I tape a few carpet threads to the receipt, which usually includes the retailer's name, address, telephone number, date and cost. The bill also itemizes the manufacturer, name, number, color, dye lot and price.

For fabric, I clip a swatch to the receipt. If the fabric can be easily confused with another fabric, I jot down where it was used on the bill of sale.

I keep an up-dated list of furniture and what I paid for insurance purposes. On major purchases, I keep clip a picture to the bill of sale so that, should I ever sell an item, I can use them both as selling tools.

In addition to my landscape architect's plan, I file the gardening articles and pictures I've collected.

If you've ever tried to touch up white paint, you know what a nightmare it can be to match the correct shade. Unless you've been religious about labeling your cans, rummaging through a dozen-plus cans of paint can be mind-boggling. I clip a paint chip sample to the receipt or brush a dab of paint directly onto the receipt and top of the can, then label each can with which room, ceiling, closet or trim I painted.

Make an effort to downsize paint cans by pouring the contents of a half-empty or three-quarters-empty paint can into a clean pint- or quart-size paint can. New cans, which can be purchased inexpensively at any paint store, will seal better and the contents, therefore, will stay fresher and last longer.

For wallpaper, I staple a cutting to the bill for reference.

Whenever I notice a low-priority task, I make a notation of it in the corresponding file. When a repairman comes to my home on a top-priority repair, I can easily present him with a comprehensive to do list.

Many of these files might be necessary for tax purposes if we ever sell our house.

Some of these files would be a valuable asset to a potential buyer if we ever sell our house.

INCOME PROPERTY DOCUMENTS

Applications	**Purchase Papers**
Assessment Cards	**Real Estate Taxes**
Insurance Policy	**Refinance Papers**
Leases	**Surveys**
Permits	**Warranties**

INCOME PROPERTY EXPENSES

Advertising	Miscellaneous
Auto and Travel	Mortgage Interest
Cleaning/Maintenance	Painting
Commissions	Real Estate Taxes
Insurance	Repairs
Legal/Professional Fees	Supplies
Licenses and Permits	Utilities

INCOME PROPERTY INCOME

Keep a separate log for each tenant reflecting the due date, amount owing, date received, amount received and your tenant's check number.

INSURANCE

Automobile Policy	Homeowner's Policy
Dental Policy	Life Policy
Health Policy	Vision Policy

In this file, as well as the following insurance files, I keep the insurance policy, literature, forms and related correspondence.

INVESTMENTS

Bonds	KEOGHs
401Ks	Mutual Funds
IRAs	Stocks

Label and separate investment literature and statements.

MEMORABILIA

This is where those scraps of memory – old documents, photos and letters – can be stored. Label each file by the person's name.

MISCELLANEOUS

Humor (cartoons and jokes)	Newspaper Clippings
Internet Printouts	Size List

Keep friends' and family size information handy to avoid returning gifts that don't fit.

NEGATIVES AND PHOTOGRAPHS

Perhaps a file cabinet is a practical place in which to store your photo albums, loose snapshots or those many envelopes containing negatives. Label your files by year for easy reference.

OFFICE SUPPLIES

Colored Paper	**Paper - Graph**
Envelopes - Letter Size	**Paper - Colored**
Envelopes - Padded/Manila	**Paper - Lined**
Index Dividers	**Paper - Tracing**
Letterhead	**Paper - Unlined**
Page Protectors	**Postage**

PERSONAL DOCUMENTS

Appraisals (antiques, art, jewelry)	**Family Tree History**
Baby Books	**Lease**
Birth Certificates	**Legal Papers**
Certificates of Title	**Marriage Certificate**
Credit Card Summary	**Military Records**
Credit Reports	**Passports**
Death Certificates	**Religious Documents**
Divorce Decree	**Safe Deposit Box List**
Drivers License (copy)	**Social Security Cards**
Emergency Instructions	**Will**

Keep duplicates in a safe deposit box or buy a fireproof safe for your irreplaceable documents.

Keep a Credit Card Summary file in case your purse or wallet is ever stolen so that you can quickly notify the proper authorities.

Although a will is a personal document and a copy of it is a key candidate for your safe deposit box, consider filing it by name which will alphabetically place it in the bottom and back of your cabinet. (See page 112.)

PETS

Label by pet's name or breed and file papers, certificates and medical records within each folder.

RECIPES

Appetizers and Dips   **Frostings and Fillings**
Biscuits and Bread   **Meats**
Cakes and Cookies   **Pies and Pastries**
Canning and Freezing   **Poultry and Stuffing**
Casseroles   **Preserves and Jellies**
Desserts   **Salads and Dressings**
Drinks and Smoothies   **Sandwiches**
Eggs and Cheese   **Sauces**
Fish and Seafood   **Soups and Stews**
Foreign Dishes   **Vegetables**

RETIREMENT

AARP   **Retirement Communities**
Benefits   **Senior Citizen Services**
Pension   **Special Service Programs**

TAXES - PENDING YEAR

Stop playing the search-and-find game with your deduction receipts. To save time doing your taxes, put all your tax receipts and statements in the place where you will be needing them next. File these back-up documents in the same order that your tax accountant's income tax workbook is written. Label each folder by page number and content. By filing your receipts directly into labeled folders, you'll save time when you prepare your taxes because the enclosed paperwork will already be in order. For example:

(Page) 6 - Wages - Commissions - Income
19 - Insurance Premiums
20 - Real Estate Taxes
21 - Charitable Contributions
22 - Tax Prep Fee
23 - Auto Registration Fee

*Retrieve remaining tax information from existing files, such as **Auto Expenses**, **Mileage**, **Medical Expenses**, and **Income Property Information**. **Dividend and Interest Income** statements usually arrive in the mail along with your W-2s and 1099s when you're already starting to prepare your taxes and, therefore, don't require separate folders.*

TAXES - PREVIOUS YEARS

Although we are legally bound to keep the past seven years' taxes, if fraud is suspected they can go back indefinitely. Keep the past two years' tax returns and receipts accessible, but box up all previous years' taxes and relegate to long-term storage. Also include any other important paperwork pertinent to that year within the corresponding box.

TRAVEL
Articles and Brochures   **Future Trips**
Car Rentals   **Incentive Programs**
Day Trips   **Maps**

*If you've accumulated scores of printed material, file by **Location** (city, state, area or country). Keep your **Tickets** in your tickler file and your **Passport** filed under Personal Documents .*

WARRANTIES AND INSTRUCTION BOOKLETS
Audio and Music Related   **Kitchen Related**
Baby Related   **Outdoor Related**
Bathroom Related   **Sports Related**
Bedroom Related   **Telephone Related**
Cameras and Camcorders   **Tools**
Clocks and Radios   **Toys**
Computer Related   **Travel Related**
Desk and Office Related   **TVs and VCRs**
Fixtures - *anything appurtenant* **Utility Room Related**
Furniture   **Vacuum Related**

Some people file these booklets in alphabetical tickler files. Because many products can be filed under more than one name, the retrieval process can be confusing. By categorizing them by kind or location, its easier to find because the middle memory process has been eliminated.

Because most warranties need evidence of purchase, it's wise to staple the original sales receipt inside each booklet's cover and keep it with the instruction booklet.

WILL AND TESTAMENT AND EMERGENCY INSTRUCTIONS

What if something happened to you and you couldn't communicate pertinent information to your loved ones or your co-workers? Are your affairs in logical, easily comprehensible order? Or would you be leaving a tangled web of mystery?

The grieving process is difficult enough without further compounding the situation by leaving someone with unfamiliar and possibly disorganized paperwork.

Perhaps this file is where personal instructions should be left in regard to what needs to be done in an emergency. Burial information could also be kept here. Your loved ones will know who to contact, what to do, where to find things, and why these things are important.

The Baker's Dozen

Regardless of content, all incoming papers fall into one of these thirteen categories:

Awaiting Response	**Errands/Outgoing**	**Receivables**
Bills	**Filing**	**Tasks**
Calendar	**Reading**	**Telephone Calls**
Computer	**Ready Reference**	**Tickler**
		– and a Round File!

When sorting mail, first open all the envelopes at one time to save repetitive movements. Discard envelopes and undesirable, unopened junk mail immediately and toss into the ROUND FILE (recycling basket).

Make immediate decisions. Don't defer them and let papers pile up. Papers that require action on your part usually, depending on your job, fall into one of the same group of categories. Observe your incoming paperwork for a week, in order to determine exactly which additional categories are applicable to your job. Try to handle similar jobs at one time rather than piecemeal. Some of these additional categories might be:

- Employee Evaluations
- Expense Reports
- Job Applications
- Monthly Reports
- Project Bids
- Travel Vouchers

If you take your work home from the office, keep your briefcase open and immediately put inside the paperwork you intend to work on at home. Place other OUTGOING papers and mail by door along with a geographic ERRANDS list. (See page 140.)

Limit yourself to only one READING basket. Each time you add an item to your pile be sure to arrange it in order of priority with the most important one on top. Keep this basket accessible so that you can easily grab and transport it to another room or area to catch up on your reading.

I often bring a pile of such papers and catalogs along with me in my car when I suspect I'll be spending a period of time waiting for my children to get out of rowing, soccer, karate, or play practice. This is also an excellent time for me to do my personal correspondence since I rarely have enough time alone to hear myself think.

Bills that need to be paid go directly into the BILLS box to be dealt with later at reasonable, periodic intervals – perhaps weekly or bimonthly. Keep them separate and apart from your other work, because they're a project in themselves.

To process bills, I immediately discard superfluous advertising inserts that come with many bills, separate the perforated bill, note the payment on the remittance advice and immediately slip it inside the envelope. I paperclip my statement to the envelope, record the due date in the upper right-hand corner of the envelope and file it in order of priority. When I pay the bill, I note the date, amount and check number somewhere on the statement, then file it. The stamp, once affixed, covers up the date notation.

Time and funds permitting, pay your bills upon receipt and eliminate the need to keep and maintain a BILLS box.

Important dates need to be entered on your CALENDAR, and details that have to be saved until a later date might need to be placed in your TICKLER file where you won't have to see them until that date. (See page 116.)

Schedules and information that need to be readily available can be added to your READY REFERENCE BOARD where they can be visible. (See page 115.)

Information that has to be entered on your computer should be set next to your COMPUTER in order of priority.

Papers that need to be filed go into the FILING box where they can accumulate until they reach a size that warrants a manageable block of time in which to file them. In other words, it doesn't make sense to keep making multiple trips to the file cabinet to file just one or two papers at a time. Rather, it would be a more efficient use of time to spend a half hour and do it all at once at the end of the day, or perhaps on a biweekly basis.

Time permitting, file your papers immediately and eliminate the need to keep and maintain this box.

Paperwork that needs addressing and that relates to an existing file should be immediately pared and clipped to its respective folder and left on your desktop as a TASK to do.

I place these files in order of priority on my desktop in staggered arrangement so their labels are visible. This stack usually receives my immediate attention.

Put papers that require a TELEPHONE CALL next to your phone in order of priority.

Have an AWAITING RESPONSE drawer or file near your telephone for papers you need to hold onto until you hear from someone else.

Keep a RECEIVABLES file (See page 116.) to keep track of the money, services, or goods due you and the person or company's name, phone number and/or address. Keep corresponding papers in the binder's pocket and cross off the information when its received.

Personal correspondence might be set on the kitchen table for the family to read and dispose of or process properly. Magazines go on the coffee table to replace previous issues which either get tossed or passed along to a friend. Usable coupons belong with the shopping list in the kitchen. Remember to occasionally weed out the out-dated coupons.

Above all, strive to get papers to their appropriate location. Be decisive and avoid the dilemma of picking up the same paper ten times and setting it down again because you don't know where it belongs.

Calendar

Keep and maintain a calendar, yearly appointment book or electronic personal organizer to avoid missing important dates and appointments.

> *I was embarrassed into purchasing a Palm Pilot when our youngest son, Adam, sought to educate me on the advantages of owning one. In retrospect, learning how to use it was relatively simple and the advantages of being able to download information to and from my computer and having internet accesses were awesome.*

Ready Reference

A convenient place to inconspicuously store necessary lists, rosters and schedules is inside a cupboard door or on the pull-out shelf of a desk.

> *Another accessible way to organize them would be to post them on a bulletin board with flat thumb tacks in staggered vertical order. Use a felt tip pen to label the visible bottom 1/4 inch of each overlapping page. In lieu of a cork board, I use two narrow corkboard memo strips placed vertically, approximately 5 inches apart.*

Receivables

As an air traffic controller regulates landing airplanes, so should you monitor your receivable transactions.

> *I keep a binder with pockets to keep track of the many things I anticipate will arrive at my home and office – checks, purchases, rebates, refunds. I date and list the dollar amount or item with a short description next to it on lined paper in sequential order. Any paperwork gets filed in the binder's pockets. Upon receipt of an item, I cross it off the list and remove the corresponding information from the pocket.*

Keep your own "receivable file" to eliminate the memory game and provide a base for all those receipts, order forms and notes flying around your house.

Telephone Log

Keep a single on-going telephone journal next to your phone and avoid coping with an assorted array of annoying and unclear messages slips, sticky notes and random slips of paper.

> *In the leather notebook next to my telephone I record most incoming and some outgoing phone numbers, names, and related information in ink and cross out in pencil when finished. I erase the pencil marks on the current page to bring the information to the front without rewriting. I date and file the pages to maintain a call history record and save retrieval time, and store related paperwork in the notebook pocket.*

Tickler Files

These expandable files comes with either alphabetical (A-Z), daily (1-31), or monthly (Jan.-Dec.) pockets. The alphabetical one is excellent for organizing clients, invoices awaiting statements, or perhaps paid bills, whereas, the numerical and monthly files feature the days of the month and months of the year and can be used to organize bills or calendar events. Each is available as a soft, closable file with a flap and string ties or as an open file with cardboard sides. The later can either be filed inside a file cabinet or stand by itself on a desk.

I prefer Globe-Weis' handsome expandable navy blue combination daily/monthly tickler which can set on a desk, stand on a shelf, or be filed in a file cabinet. I use its daily section, labeled 1 - 31, to store paperwork I need to refer to in a timely fashion that month.

Perhaps I'll keep directions for driving on a school field trip here. An early-purchased birthday card for the 14th might be filed under the 12th to allow time for mailing. I might also include a reminder where I hid the gift!

A wedding invitation for the 30th could be filed in the previous week to allow time to shop for a gift. I might file fabric samples that need to be returned the day I go to the city.

When I reach the last day of the month in my daily tickler file, I empty out the following month's file from my monthly tickler file and file under the appropriate day in my daily tickler file.

I use the tickler's monthly section, labeled from January to December, to store papers I need to see in months other than the present. If I am finished working on a particular file and need to wait for something else to happen before I need it next, and that most probably won't happen until the following month, I will more than likely file it in that month's file.

I keep a card in each of the twelve monthly files to flag the birthdays and anniversaries that fall within that particular month. This is also where I leave myself reminder notes of long-term appointments and dates, such as doctor appointments every two years, real estate and business license renewals every so many years and

117

*certain warranty expiration dates. I leave a reminder
in that month's folder and ignore it until the pertinent
year.*

Literature Sorters

Cardboard, formica and wooden literature sorters provide separate spaces in which to store reams of paper where they are protected on three sides and easily accessible. I recommend investing in a solid wooden or formica literature sorter as opposed to one with weaker cardboard shelves.

Years ago, I paid $2 at a garage sale for a brand new cardboard sweater organizer which sets sideways upon the top of my four-drawer file cabinet and my children and I use as a literature sorter. It has nine shelves in which my business stationery fits perfectly. It has enabled me to empty out several desk drawers and clear valuable desk-top work areas. These are the reams of paper and various supplies that I usually store there.

• *Letterhead stationery*	• *Construction paper*
• *Plain paper*	• *Sheet protectors*
• *Plain paper with holes*	• *Folder covers*
• *Lined paper*	• *Spiral notebooks*

Literature sorters that conveniently fit beneath your computer or printer are now available in colors that match most computers. These are optimal, because they provide a selection of about six types of papers at your fingertips while you are sitting at your computer terminal. And, because they are placed beneath existing equipment, they don't take up any additional desktop work space.

Office Organizers

These can be purchased as either horizontal or vertical organizers. They enable you to store papers by using a minimum of work space.

Rethink how you use your work surfaces. Do you have stacks of papers covering your desktop, tables, kitchen counters and clothes drier?

These areas ideally should be cleared of clutter in order to serve the purpose for which they are intended.

Remember: Each paper takes up approximately 8 1/2 by 11 inches of space or 93.5 square inches when placed flat on a desk. If you store the same paper upright in a vertical file you only take up 1/32 of an inch by 11 inches!

Vertical desk organizers hold folders upright just like an open file cabinet drawer. They work best for me whenever I'm inundated with assorted projects that I need to keep accessible. I categorize them, put them in folders, label them and file by priority. By putting folders on end, I can easily access them and save valuable work area. I always file projects in order of priority.

I keep a seven-tier horizontal desk organizer on top of my desk for the projects I am currently working on that require keeping a lot of paperwork. I often change the labels to suit my workload. For example, in December, I designate a shelf for my income tax and, upon finishing my tax return, file it away by year and then use the shelf for something else.

This is also where I keep and maintain my basic files. (See page 102.) I limit all my paperwork to just one area in my home to minimize legwork and to better utilize my time.

The Desk Pad

Translucent desk pads can nearly double the usable surface area of nearly any desk by providing visible access to a variety of papers.

For handy reference, keep a small calendar, chart of accounts, telephone numbers, rosters, schedules, or perhaps some special photographs beneath its protective clear pad.

Working on Project Files

Each project file should have a cover sheet attached to the front. Keep an on-going dated history of your progress to establish a paper trail to prove your efforts to your superiors and provide an informational background for your successor. Note telephone calls, meetings, and record your work progress. If constructive, record time spent in the margin.

A project calendar sheet will help keep your project on schedule by displaying meetings, periodic deadlines and anticipated completion date. Be consistent and always file your newest paper on the top inside each file to minimize rifling through loose papers. Notes or post-it notes on which you jot down a thought, idea, or reminder should, once you are back at your desk, be either attached to their corresponding file or the information should be transferred appropriately.

By using color folders, it is easier to spot important projects.

Perhaps you could use a red folder for financial information, a blue one for correspondence and a yellow one for project-related names, telephone numbers and cover sheet.

Pressboard partition folders with optional closable pockets in back can house up to six classifications. Each of the multiple sections are equipped with reinforced fasteners. This clever folder is perfect for tracking diversified projects.

Whenever a file is removed from the file cabinet, particularly in an office where there are several people who have access to the files, there is always the chance that the file will be misplaced or lost. To avoid such unsettling situations, consider creating a system whereby the files must be signed out.

Likewise, when a file is returned to the file cabinet, there exists the possibility that it might be misfiled. By making one person responsible for the filing, this common pitfall can be minimized.

Desk Drawers for Projects

Use excess desk drawer space to contain and limit unwieldy projects.

I thin out my decorating catalogs whenever they overflow their exclusive desk drawer.

Junk Mail Junkie

The average family receives about four and a half pounds of junk mail weekly and spends about seven minutes a day processing it which, over a period of 70 years, translate into four months of wasted time. A person who spends ten minutes a day loses six months, and one who lingers twenty minutes a day loses up to one year of his or her life during the same 70-year period.

In desperation to cure a junk mail junkie who was indecisive about tossing junk mail and predisposed to saving it, I told her the solicitor was attempting to rob her life and she was willingly forfeiting her precious time.

To have your name and address removed from direct marketing mailing lists, write to:

The Mail Preference Service
Direct Marketing Association
P. O. Box 9008
Farmingdale, NY   11735-9008

Be discriminating. Don't be victimized by unsolicited junk mail.

Keep the Home Fires Burning

Every day of their lives, our early ancestors faced the daily dilemma – how to keep their home fires burning and still find time to hunt for food. Although their quest for food was of paramount importance, their secondary needs also needed addressing. It's understandable that, while the stronger mate searched for food, the weaker mate remained at their shelter to provide those necessities – keeping a fire burning for warmth and for cooking purposes, preparing food, making clothing and tending to offspring.

In many ways, our lives are patterned after early man. Food, shelter, clothing and child rearing are still of primary importance. The necessity to go out and forage a living remains offset by daily housekeeping activities. There is a delicate balance between the two co-existing responsibilities – the hunter cannot hunts unless he is fed, rested and dressed warmly, and the family cannot survive without food – the lack of one duty ultimately affects the other, and vice versa.

This theory can be paralleled to our daily workload. New business is the lifeblood of any enterprise. It must be counterbalanced with efficient processing of information, completion of projects, correspondence, filing and follow-up procedures to stay current and thrive.

With the downsizing of personnel in most companies, this marriage of responsibilities is increasingly becoming the responsibility of the individual employee. We must try to forge ahead and yet we are responsible for the other less-recognized, but equally valuable, duties. With an organized and functional office, we are more apt to achieve our goals and expectations.

Like our forbearers, we must strive to put the meat on our tables, yet be mindful of keeping our home fires burning – or rather the home files churning – to survive our strive and succeed in life.

YOUR OFFICE
AND OTHER TOOLS

- CHAPTER X -

YOUR OFFICE AND OTHER TOOLS

The Advantage of Having an Organized Office

Having your office organized is not an end in itself, but rather a vehicle to take you to where you need to get. A functional system is a true reflection of your mental picture of organization and is a tool which, if consistently used with the proper techniques, will enable you to achieve your goals.

Perhaps you're already using some of the ideas in this book without being consciously aware of it. If you're a logical thinker who approaches work and solves problems systematically then, hopefully, you're already able to evaluate random incoming work by determining your priorities and approaching them sequentially.

Dynamic Workplaces

More and more progressive companies are learning the value of judging their workers by their *results* and not by their *appearance*. They are privileging workers by allowing them to decide for themselves when, where and how they work. The main theory is that when people have a choice, they are inclined to be more productive.

Many companies give their employees the freedom to come and go as they please without requiring definite work hours. Some workers prefer to occasionally work out of their homes, some prefer working flexible hours out of their office. Whatever their choice, they are judged by their results and not by punching the time clock of a baby-sitting company.

Environments where people are treated as adults and allowed to make their own decisions foster trust. Employees that can balance work with their private lives are more apt to be content. Workers who know that their company is supportive of all their needs demonstrate loyalty.

Blind acceptance of the cookie cutter office is being challenged. Many companies today are empowering their workers to reshape their individual work spaces. By having a choice in the matter, workers are more inclined to create an environment that's custom-tailored to fulfilling their needs.

In addition to physical changes in the workplace, there is the secondary consideration of the social change. How workers interact with each other is key to their productivity. By enabling people to decide for themselves who they need to collaborate with and where certain activities need to be conducted, companies can help employees to operate more efficiently and, therefore, to be more productive.

Companies and departments need areas for concentrating on individual work as well as gathering places for casual exchanges of ideas or for formal business meetings.

Office Etiquette

Discuss interoffice etiquette with your co-workers. Be aware of the differences in personalities and moods within the office. People who prefer working in solitude, with minimal or no interruptions often have a closed-door policy, while others have an open-door policy. Neither is right or wrong. Whatever works for the individual at the time is best. But be aware of the subtle signals co-workers may be sending you about their stress levels on any particular day and, if possible, honor their wishes.

Those who have difficulty staying on track, should consider arranging a schedule for making telephone calls, handling incoming mail, reading reports, and working on projects. If co-workers know that certain periods of the day are better than others, chances are they will respect your wishes. If you require solitude, communicate your desires to others about respecting your closed door, but anticipate occasional interruptions regarding matters of importance to others.

Commanding the Room

The next time you enter your office, look at it objectively and be conscious of your first impression. Ask yourself if you find your office visually pleasing. Evaluate whether the room's contents appear balanced. Judge how functional or organized it appears at first glance.

In deciding on your furniture placement, start with the largest piece of furniture and work your way down to the smallest pieces. Position your desk so that you will be able to see who is entering your office. Having command of the room shows authority and control.

Also take full advantage of the scenery. Since you're going to be spending a great deal of time at your desk, you might prefer a view out a window to a desk facing a wall. Landscaped views can relax and inspire. In a windowless office, use your imagination. Perhaps a window-framed nature poster or trompe l'oeil would give the illusion of exterior access.

Make your office furniture work for you. Create a mini environment from your desk chair. Position a credenza behind your desk chair to double your accessible, functional work surface. Your credenza can also hold reference literature, equipment or files available to you by a mere swivel of your chair. Likewise, a side table can expand your desktop by providing a continuous work surface with just minimal movement required by you. This impressive-looking arrangement can be highly functional.

Surround yourself with the tools of your trade, and remember to use horizontal – as well as vertical – areas. For example, if you often use the file cabinet or bookcase, then they belong near your work area. Consider positioning a bank of two-drawer file cabinets behind your desk with a flat work surface on top. An overhead bookcase would maximize the use of the otherwise neglected vertical space.

If your work place is pleasant as well as functional then you're apt to enjoy your work, have a more positive attitude and, in turn, be more productive.

Desks

Make sure that your desk fits your needs and provides you with an adequate work surface area. Starting with the largest pieces, position your equipment in logical and comfortable locations.

Because I am right-handed, I prefer my telephone on the left side of my desk so that the cord stays to the left of me and never crosses over my writing arm and writing surface.

I keep my calculator on my right so I can easily operate it with my right hand and have an unobstructed view of the paper directly in front of me in the center of my desk without having to look over my arm.

Take note of the area above your desk. If your desk faces a wall, an overhead bookcase or literature organizer might be suitable for reference materials and frequently used supplies.

Some newer desk arrangements have clever, space-saving file cabinets which pull out from under the desk and provide an additional arm of work surface. By the same token, computer desks which have recessed areas for the computer and monitor, plus designated pull-out drawers for the printer, keyboard and mouse pad, can free the desktop of clutter to further enhance the total usability of the surface work space.

I cannot stress enough the need to have a desk with adequate work surface and storage area. Ideally, your desktop should hold only the items and papers you are presently working on and be cleared at the end of the day. Think of your desk as a tool and equip it in such a fashion that its contents are instrumental in the fulfillment of your work tasks.

The Center Drawer

Center desk drawers should always contain small, miscellaneous useful items.

- Pens / pencils / markers
- Rubber bands / paper clips
- Staples / staple remover
- Erasers / white out
- Sticky notes / stamps
- Scissors / rulers
- Glue / glue stick

These items are universally standard occupants of most every desk drawer. It's an unwritten code. They migrate from various parts of the world and take up residence in desk drawers. And not just any desk drawer – just the center desk drawer.

Now, you have to be very careful of these aliens. When they first move in, they are very orderly. But, if you don't keep an eye on them – bedlam! And they don't work and play well amongst themselves.

What they prefer, actually, is to live in segregated little places. You need to separate the various groups, so they can co-exist in peaceful harmony and be readily available when called upon for active duty.

To arrange and separate these items, you can either buy the molded plastic organizers, compartmentalized inserts or just use an assortment of shallow boxes, such as checkbook boxes, stationery boxes, or candy and soap boxes with molded plastic inserts.

I save various shallow boxes and position them so that the entire drawer is tightly divided into multiple sections. I keep the drawer supplied with small pads of paper, pencils, pens, erasers, markers, stapler, staples, paper clips, a paper clip remover, a calculator, stamps, rubber bands and rubber fingers for sorting. Such simple box arrangements utilize 100% of your drawer space as opposed to store-bought, molded-plastic organizers that contain little hills separating shallow valleys for supplies and are rarely the exact size of a desk drawer.

Before discarding them, take a second look at molded-plastic inserts from soap and candy boxes. Occasionally, they can be used to separate small items in drawers. I found an ideal organizer for embroidery thread is the formed-plastic interior from a box of chocolate confectionery sticks.

Credenzas

Side tables or rear credenzas look particularly professional and provide extra work surface or enable you to clear your desk by providing housing for your equipment. With such an arrangement, a swivel chair is a necessity.

Credenzas are excellent for holding reference materials, equipment, and office supplies on top and inside their doored cupboards. A carefully chosen work of art might soften the decor.

Functional Project Areas

Examine your present work areas and determine if they're set up logically. Identify each area's function and endeavor to group related activities together. By doing so, you eliminate the memory game of searching out the various files, folders, binders, etc., to complete specific tasks.

If you have an extensive project, consider devoting an entire table to handle its paperwork. Perhaps it will warrant its own file cabinet or drawer, if you will continue to maintain it. If it's a project that you're preparing for someone else and eventually pass along in its entirety, then either a portable cardboard or plastic file box might be more feasible.

Bookcases

Previously mentioned in Chapter V, on page 39, bookcases are equally versatile in the home as in the office. They serve the same purpose whether they're built-in or free-standing bookcases, with or without doors, or simple wall-mounted, open shelving. Besides being a reservoir for books, bookcases can serve as a handsome display for eclectic collections.

A client of mine was frustrated over the ever-expanding volume of books, binders and catalogs in her converted-bedroom office. By building 7 shelves inside her 6-foot wide, 8-foot high closet, we were able to provide 48 linear feet of shelving. This configuration accommodated 24 bankers boxes, 12 feet of shelving for books and binders, 6 feet for catalogs and reference materials, plus 6 feet of open shelving for a work surface. The closet's double doors could shut its contents out of sight.

A trick to determine how many bookcases you need, is to take a tape measurer and measure the spines of all your books, binders, catalogs, and magazines. Divide their combined widths by the lengths of your shelving to determine the minimum number of shelves you will require. Always allow for expansion.

Supplies

Office supplies are a necessary expense which are usually taken for granted. Most companies provide a never-ending supply of nearly anything you want. If they don't have what you want, they'll order it for you. Office supply expenses take a big chunk out of a company's profit. If it's a lean year, they can pick the bones clean.

How many times have you gone through your desk drawers and come across dozens of ballpoint pens and half-used pads of paper you no longer need? Don't throw them away. Recycle.

Once a month, schedule a Supply Pick-Up Day when a clerk visits each office carrying a big box or pushing a cart on wheels to pick up surplus supplies.

> *Remember the cigarette girls in the 50's with their boxes of cigarettes? This is the reverse principle. Instead of calling out, "Cigarettes! Cigarettes!", the supply pick-up person would call out, "Supplies! Supplies!" People might even be willing to pay to have their surplus supplies taken off their hands.*

Another idea would be to leave a large box in a central area to collect excess office supplies and/or resource materials. Collected supplies should periodically be returned to the supply room.

Consider starting a supply "orphanage" cabinet, for your floor or building.

Doing this will:

- Help you clean up your desk, removing superfluous items.

- Give you more usable space, so you can function
  more efficiently.

- Save perhaps thousands of dollars annually or
  your division or department, to increase profits.

Duplicate Supplies

Keep duplicate supplies together with the tasks that require them.

If, for example, the only time you use your pocket calculator is when you do your bank reconciliation, then keep it on top of your canceled checks. The theory is that after you check off your canceled checks from your statement the next thing you habitually do is file them away. When the calculator is precisely where you need it, you eliminate the time spent collecting it from a different location.

Other supplies you may need for particular projects include pencils, pens, markers, stamps, scissors, letter openers, rubber bands, staplers and labels.

In a household, storing utensils like measuring spoons and scoops together with baking or laundry supplies can be real time savers. Leaving measuring cups inside bags of dry pet food would diminish time spent cleaning up spills.

Keep duplicate personal items where you use them, too. For example, keep a set of make-up in your purse or car. Put cleaning supplies in each bathroom. A copy of your personal telephone numbers would be convenient in your car.

Pencil and Paper

Do you sometimes have a great idea or remember something you have to do – then forget to follow through on it? To avoid this situation, keep a pen and note pad on your person to jot down your thoughts and ideas. Additionally, keep them in various places in and around your home, office, and automobile.

At Work – Keep a paper and pencil near all telephones, on the tables in the cafeteria, and near the vending machines.

If you have metal bathroom stalls at the office, then attach a strip of magnetic backing to small pads of paper and stick them on the walls. You might tie a string to a pen or pencil and tape the other end to the back of the pad of paper. If your walls are not metal, then attach a strip of adhesive or velcro instead.

At Home – Stick a pencil and paper in your pocket when you go outside to garden or take a walk. Keep them near the TV, on your night stand and in the bathroom.

One of my children received a set of crayon soap for a birthday and it has come in handy more than once for jotting down ideas while in the shower. I suppose regular crayons might work too, although they might be a bit more difficult to scrub off.

In Your Automobile – You can keep pens and pads of paper in the door pocket, or buy a unit that attaches to your dashboard.

For convenience sake, I often use a small, voice-activated tape recorder to note thoughts for later.

Tape Recorders

Tape recorders are ideal in many situations and I encourage everyone to make a habit of carrying a small one at all times. In addition to dictating your correspondence, you can use a tape recorder in place of a pen and pencil to make notes to yourself.

I use a tape recorder to collect my thoughts and, when I am back in my office, I process them. This could mean I make additions to my telephone list or errand list, record dates on my calendar, record information on my computer, update a file, etc. In other words, to send these bits of information on the first leg of their journey, get the information to the place it belongs right away.

One of the places where I do not recommend using a tape recorder is when you're in a rest room stall. People really begin to wonder about you when you are in there alone and start talking to yourself.

Sticky Notes

Sticky notes, when used discriminately, are positive little tools. When overused, however, they can work to your detriment.

A client, anxious to be organized, covered his walls with these handy little reminders. Note: Sticky notes are not wallpaper!

Many of his notes were to remind himself to either make a telephone call or perform a task. By transferring his notes to two on-going lists – a telephone call list and a to do list – he managed to eliminate dozens of sticky notes from his office. By consolidating the information, my client was able to take his reminders with him whenever he left his office.

Use a variety of colors and sizes, to flag different projects. To avoid paging back through literature, use stickies as page markers and jot down notes on the exposed portion.

For a clean look for your books setting on bookshelves, position sticky notes on the right or left of each page and not at the top where they would be visible.

Color Tabs

To diminish misfiling, use color codes to differentiate groups of files by attaching color tabs to the top of your manila folders. Misplaced files will be easily spotted at a glance.

Medical offices often use these codes for organizing their patients' files.

OFFICE PAPERWORK AND PROCEDURES

- CHAPTER XI -

OFFICE PAPERWORK
AND PROCEDURES

Paper Weight

According to *The New York Times*, the crisis at Three Mile Island might have been avoided if the manufacturers of the nuclear reactor had been more conscientious in the processing of their paperwork.

> *"Officials of the Babcock & Wilsox Company conceded today that they had failed to take proper heed of warning last year. They said the warnings, contained in memoranda written by assistants, had been sent to the wrong people, and had been subordinated to more pressing matters . . ."*

Another tragedy that might have been avoided was the sinking of the British luxury passenger liner, the Titanic, and the resulting loss of 1,513 lives after an iceberg ripped a 300-foot gash in its right side on its maiden voyage in April of 1912. The *Encyclopedia Britannica* quotes:

> *"Although general manager, Ismay, was first blamed and Captain Smith was cited, it was Phillips, the senior wireless radio operator, who ignored three transmissions from other ships that had previously traveled through the area and sent warning of the presence of icebergs in the area."*

The power of the word. The word on paper. How easily it can get misdirected, mislaid, or forgotten. It's amazing how such a trivial piece of paper can have an impact of such gigantic proportions.

How can we avoid disastrous situations in our own lives? Perhaps a good place to start is by listening to our consciences. That edgy, there's-just not-enough-time feeling, constant interruptions, incoming papers exceeding outgoing papers and that clammy, helpless, drowning feeling are all symptoms that we need to be aware of every day. Constant roller-coaster feelings eventually result in diminishing personal confidence, which is a forerunner of incompetency.

When people appear to be neat and well-organized, on the other hand, their orderliness promotes confidence and implies good judgment, and success.

Attacking Paperwork in the Office

According to a recent Gallup survey, 70% of employees of Fortune 1000 companies feel overwhelmed by the volume of daily messages and documents they receive. Here is the average number of messages each worker fields daily:

- 31.8 phone calls
- 6.0 sticky notes
- 13.6 e-mail messages
- 5.1 telephone message slips
- 11.2 voice mail messages
- 3.9 pager messages
- 8.8 faxed documents

When you count phone calls, mail, e-mail, voice mail, memos, and faxes received and sent each day, they average 178 communications per worker. In addition, employees process an average of five meetings each week – and executives attend nine meetings per week.

Despite years of predictions of the "paperless office," the reverse is actually true because they forgot to consider the printer, fax and copy machine. People today are more inclined to call and send messages for trivial things, resulting in an enormous amount of superfluous information to sort through to get to relevant information. Because communication traffic is constantly increasing, frustration over managing the volume is likewise growing. Being able to sort through the glut of paperwork and deal with important issues and having access to the right information at the right time is of primary importance.

Mismanagement of paper disables your ability to function efficiently and produces missed opportunities, incomplete projects, lost information, wasted time, frustration and profit loss.

Grand Central Station

Keeping on track is easy when you're dealing with just a single track; however, most of us, unfortunately, do not work under such idealistic conditions.

More than likely, your working pattern is fragmented because of sporadic interruptions of others through various media, such as impromptu conversations with co-workers, meetings, telephone calls, voice mail, mail, special deliveries, faxes, and on-line messages. When you think about it, it's a wonder we can accomplish anything at all!

You could compare each day in a large office to rush hour at Grand Central Station. An office and its employees, with their pressing schedules and goals, are like a busy commuter station with so many train lines arriving and departing within so much time and on just so many tracks. Finding a workable schedule to satisfy all needs is of utmost importance. Sticking with it is imperative.

Evaluate your success the end of each day in trying to keep on track. Ask yourself, "Was today an exercise in staying afloat or treading water like crazy? Did this day incorporate my managerial skills or descend to martyrdom? Did I display fortitude or futility? Were my successes the result of skill or just dumb luck?"

The Complex Individual

Every day of your work week, you are confronted with a variety of things that you need to deal with. Each day's work is a compilation of multiple, miscellaneous fragments.

This is a diagram of a typical worker's concerns on any particular day:

Daily Routines:

Basic Necessities
(sleep - shower - dress - eat - drive)

Work (daily routine plus projects)   Errands (pick up cleaning; buy gift)

Communication (phone; fax; mail)   Obligations (chauffeur children)

Meetings (9:30; lunch; 3:00)   Appointments (doctor; dinner date)

Leisure
(tennis, jog, read)

Goals and Ambitions
(advancement - home - car - trip - college - wedding - retirement)

139

In other words, you have a lot of things going on inside your head each day, before you even get to work. It's not a matter of just showing up at the office, sitting there for eight hours and doing the same thing all day long.

Success is a continual juggling act. You have to keep things moving if you don't want to drop the ball.

Categorizing Responsibilities

All the things we need to attend to each day can be logically grouped together in the following manner:

- Appointments - Meetings - Obligations (with time requirements)

- Telephone Calls

- Errands - Obligations (without time requirements)

- Projects

Your **Appointment** Calendar should be consulted the day before the appointment, so you can prepare all necessary, related files or paperwork. Your schedule should rest on top of the pertinent files, which should be stacked in order of their time requirements and their respective importance.

Telephone Calls should be noted on an on-going list. The list should contain names and phone numbers of people you plan to call, together with the reason for each call. Beneath this list should be the necessary files that pertain to the phone calls. Any notes you take should be logged within the corresponding file.

Errands should be listed on an on-going page, as well. Think about keeping this list in map form, rather than on an itemized list. Cross off errands as you complete them, and add new ones. This way of listing things is also ideal for shopping at grocery stores and shopping at malls, will save you time and energy, and help you visualize other shopping possibilities.

Your **Projects** or Things To Do List are also on-going lists of what you need to focus and work on. Keep this list in order of importance. Cross off items when the task has been completed and add new ones at the bottom. *Anything* you have to do should be on this list. This list should be a true reflection of your memory.

Getting a Jump on the Day

Before leaving the office each night, take a few moments to plan the following day. Write down your telephone call list and numbers, your appointments and errands, as well as the anticipated time on your daily planner. Organize the files and materials you need for each appointment so everything is ready the first thing in the morning.

Having these things ready will give you an edge on the day, especially when the telephone is ringing off the hook and co-workers are pressing to talk with you.

Prioritizing Tasks

Every time you add a paper to an existing stack of paperwork or file, prioritize by putting the most critical paper on top and less important papers beneath in order of importance. This minor task is probably the most significant habit you could possibly cultivate in order to achieve maximum efficiency.

Occasionally, however, you must address those items that keep slipping down to the bottom of the pile. A good way is to simply turn the pile over and direct your attention to the one that is now on top.

Such deferred little nuisances tend to create psychological black holes in our minds. The negative feelings they instill can undermine a person's confidence. Often, people expend more energy contemplating a task than actually doing it.

Making Telephone Calls

Try to make all telephone calls within one block of time so your day is less fragmented. Keep reading material on hand for when you're placed on hold or waiting to be connected.

This is also a good time to do small, automatic manual tasks such as opening your mail, straightening your desk or drawers, sharpening your pencils, removing receipts from your wallet, or putting canceled checks in numerical order.

Business Meetings

Think twice about calling a meeting. Can the same things be accomplished by memo, e-mail, or teleconference to save time? Weigh the cost benefits. Is the meeting worth the expense of workers' loss of productivity? Take into account the time spent away from their work centers, plus the extra time it takes people to get back on track.

Define the purpose of your meeting, prepare an agenda with time estimates, and stick with it. If workers are aware of time constraints, they'll be less likely to bring up unimportant or unrelated matters. A flip chart or white board will help people stay focused on the issues.

Evaluate periodic meetings for their relevancy. What might have worked last year doesn't necessarily apply this year. Should a portion of the subject matter be deleted? Or expanded? Can related subjects be included, or, can two separate meetings be combined? Is the time frame and location realistic and convenient? Whose presence is necessary? Who else could benefit from receiving the information?

A sure gimmick, to insure a quick meeting and an alert audience, is to hold it in a location where there are no chairs. People are more alert when they're standing up and they're less inclined to linger afterward.

Reading Time

Make the time you spend doing bulk reading a pleasant experience. Create the right setting with a comfortable chair, reading lamp and perhaps an ottoman and comforter. Keep a dictionary on hand as well as paper, pencil, highlighter, bookmark and sticky notes.

Limit the size of your reading file or box. When it grows to unrealistic proportions, then it's time to either spend some serious time reading or thin it out and learn to be more discriminating. Avoid burying reading by occasionally turning the pile over.

Take advantage of various times during the day in which you can do a little reading, such as during meals, or in a taxi, train or plane. Other available opportunities might include the time you spend waiting. Whether you wait in a car, on the telephone or in a waiting room, these empty minutes can add up to a reasonable block of time. Taking advantage of these small chunks will also free up your leisure time.

Newspapers and Magazines

Evaluate the importance or necessity of your subscriptions. Tear out important articles you need to read and toss the remainder whenever feasible. Avoid repetitively paging through literature by referring directly to the table of contents for articles of interest.

Incoming Reports

Be aware of how many reports you receive each month. Determine how much of the information you receive is relevant. If none of it is, then have yourself removed from the routing list. If only part of it is, then request that portion of the report be sent to you instead.

By selectively choosing incoming documents, you'll save time and energy – both your own because you don't have to wade through irrelevant information, and the preparer's. Plus, you eliminate the office expenses associated with unnecessary document preparation.

If the sender of the report indicates it is unrealistic to provide special handling, then cut out the section that is applicable to your needs and discard the remainder. By eliminating the bulk of the report, you will not be cluttering up your files with superfluous papers.

Outgoing Reports

Determine the proportion of time spent preparing reports, as opposed to the amount of time spent doing productive work. Evaluate the importance of each outgoing report. Ask recipients if they need the information it contains. Solicit people's ideas for improvement and where or to whom the information should be directed.

Whenever possible, consolidate reports. It's more economical to send out a single mailing and, for the receiver, it is usually easier to deal with one report than multiple pieces of paper. Highlight key points and avoid being too wordy.

Question the time intervals between reports. Should a report be sent monthly or bimonthly, weekly or biweekly? Determine whether or not a report should be deleted altogether. Unnecessary reports sent out of habit can slowly drain an office or company of profits.

Routing Reports

When you route paperwork for review by colleagues, put your name at the bottom and an expected date of return. File a copy in your tickler file on the anticipated return date to verify that you sent the information, or to enable you to trace it. By requiring recipients to initial and date the report next to their name on the routing slip, procrastinators can be readily identified.

Another alternative is to post periodic reports and require your staff to read, initial and date them within an allotted time period. This system works best if employees spend time working outside of their office.

Visual Reports

Some information is more easily understandable when it's illustrated by a chart or graph rather than lengthy text. When comparing production or profits to previous periods, visual information can be perceived at a glance. Updated visual reports replace previous business graphics and minimize space in the filing cabinet.

Time-Efficient Correspondence

When you have a lot of correspondence that requires a similar response, prepare form letters and insert the date, name and address.

Another possibility is a standardized checklist form. For letters requiring specialized written responses, prepare base paragraphs on your computer and mix and match them by using the cut and paste edit functions. Whenever possible, condense information into half-page forms or postcards. Some in-house correspondence which requires a response can be be simplified by jotting a note at the bottom of the page.

Mailing Lists

Computerized mailing labels, or even pre-printed and pre-stamped envelopes or postcards save time and money. Window envelopes eliminate the duplication of typing the name and address on form correspondence. Rubber stamps can also be used for mailing purposes.

Rubber Stamps

Rubber stamps can be used for routine messages. Papers which require multiple actions can be condensed on a single stamp. Progressive information – such as date received, date due, date paid, amount paid, check number, account number and approved by – can be recorded on a single stamp.

Delivery Services

Take advantage of delivery services in your area. You'll save time, energy, gas and wear and tear on your car – plus, you'll minimize the amount of time when you're susceptible to having a traffic accident.

Delivery services available in your area might include dry cleaning, office supplies, dairy products, groceries, flowers, drugs, wine and liquor.

Another possibility is shopping from catalogs. The value of your time usually surpasses the amount you pay for shipping and handling.

If You Give a Mouse a Cookie

Just about anyone who has a child is familiar with Laura Joffe Numeroff's book, *If You Give a Mouse a Cookie*, which delightfully demonstrates the domino-effect theory. She writes about the effects of the single action of merely giving a cookie to a mouse.

First, he'll want a glass of milk. Next, a straw. Then a napkin to clean off his whiskers, and so on and so forth. Likewise, be aware of the sequential nature of tasks. Evaluate the entire progression, and bypass unnecessary steps if at all possible.

Repetitive Tasks

Be aware of repetitive tasks and strive to simplify them. For example, recurring duties like paying the rent, recording automatic bank withdrawals, gathering information for a monthly report, or sending out billings can be noted on 3 x 5 cards and moved through the monthly tickler file to serve as reminders.

Be Consistent

Learn to be a creature of good habits in the office as well as in the home.

If your expenses need to be charged to different accounts, it would be wise to immediately jot down the reference on the back of each charge slip while the information is still fresh in your mind. When you return to your home or office, make a habit of emptying your pockets of all those little bank charge receipts as soon as you walk in the door.

Perhaps you have a drawer or decorative container you can quickly and easily drop them into where they can stay safe, out of sight, until the end of the month, when your statement arrives.

When your credit card statement arrives, sequentially match and check off charges and credits and staple them to the back of each page. If you need to break down the numbers for tax purposes, note on each line which account is to be charged, total each account and record the totals at the bottom of the last page of the statement.

Keep an on-going cover sheet on each working file to keep track of its history. Record the date and time of conversations, telephone calls, correspondence and events. Attach incoming and outgoing correspondence to the appropriate file, to reflect the sequential order indicated on the cover sheet.

EDUCATION AND MAINTENANCE

- CHAPTER XII -

EDUCATION AND MAINTENANCE

Learning from the Start

When selecting a preschool for your child, consider what responsibilities are expected of your child. Avoid chaotic institutions. Children, like adults, are happier working in an uncluttered environment which eliminates distractions and anxieties and promotes concentration and creativity.

The Montessori preschool my children attended embodies my principles regarding orderliness. Everything has a place. All projects are self-contained in a box or basket and neatly lined up on shelves around the room. After an activity is selected, it is taken to either a mat on the floor or to a table. Upon completion of the chosen task, the child is required to return it to its original place. This practice exemplifies what I taught my children at home. That is, play with whatever you like, but kindly put it back in its appropriate place when you are done.

Small children learn by example how to make their beds, straighten their rooms and put their clothes, toys and books away. As an incentive, make it a nightly ritual before that bedtime story. Little ones quickly realize that the shorter the clean-up time, the longer the story time, and will be more apt to do their chores with enthusiasm or perhaps even beforehand.

Keep toy collections in separate baskets, boxes or drawers. Everything should have a place. When a new toy arrives on the scene, decide together what would be an ideal new home for it. Consider whether it's something you want to be on display or hidden from view. Should it be easily accessible or stored on an upper shelf for safe keeping? If there are parts to it, can they be stored inside or is it necessary to provide a container?

When my children's rooms are particularly neat when they go to bed, the Room Fairy leaves shiny pennies on their beds and all around the room on their carpet while they sleep.

What Can I Do to Help?

Teach young family members to become aware of their environment and their place within it.

In 1987, when our fourth child, Adam, was born, Matthew was two years old and still toddling around the house, Jessica was five years old and in afternoon preschool, and Joshua, age seven, was in first grade on the opposite side of town. In order to get our children to and from school at four different times each day, do the shopping and run various errands all around town, just getting out of the house – with diaper bags, bottle bags, assorted clothing, toys, snacks, backpacks, strollers, blankets and books – was something of a daily challenge.

Within a few months, Matthew turned three and was delighted to attend his big sister's preschool, too. Of course, that particular class met twice a week in the mornings, which entailed another two different drop off and pick up times, which brought the minimum number of trips to town up to six and often necessitated packing lunch for five.

My husband and I are truly blessed with four beautiful and kind children. Our children learned at an early age to be aware of others' needs. I explained to them how overwhelming it could be for one person to do everything for everybody and gave them concrete examples of what they could do to help. They learned to "open their eyes" to see what needed to be done and, after doing what was obvious to them, to further offer their help by asking, "What can I do to help?"

Now they are older and constantly amaze me with their capacity for kindness to others.

Good character traits learned at an early age usually carry over into adolescence, then adulthood, to create aware, responsible and caring citizens, spouses and parents.

Felix Ungers

Every so often, a child is born with an innate sense of orderliness. Although compulsion for perfection is to be admired, be aware that rigid, self-imposed high expectations can result in frequent frustrations. While your child may exhibit a natural tendency toward orderliness, this doesn't necessarily mean that the level he or she seeks is easily attained.

Born to be Wild

Getting messy older children to keep up their rooms often becomes increasingly difficult. They tend to develop their own standards of orderliness. Positive results of previously effective methods by parents eventually fade and become pathetically transparent. That intimidating "look" that worked so well when they were two feet shorter will only get you a snicker now. Basically, these messy types often don't care about their rooms and don't see why you should either.

Convincing older children to maintain their rooms is an art form in itself. With many, you can talk until you are blue in the face and they will continue doing precisely what they want to do. I have one word of advice at this point – *Leverage!*

Using Leverage

Getting some teenagers to take an active interest in their bedrooms as opposed to their outside world is forever a challenge.

> *I've been known to try, "Okay, now that you are a teenager, I'm going to stop treating you like a child. I'm not going to nag you anymore about keeping your room in order." This is always met with pride and appreciation. Give this time to sink in and casually mention on your way out of the room, "However, you do realize that when Brian calls on the weekend, you'll only be allowed to go if you've maintained your room throughout the week."*

One thing, however, I have learned as a parent is to be flexible.

Although the results are not as I envisioned, on many a Saturday morning I hear the telephone ringing, followed by the hum of the vacuum upstairs, followed by the sound of heavy feet running down the stairs. Then there's the usual dialogue: "Can I go to Brian's?" "Is your room clean"? "Yes." "Okay, you can go." "Thanks, Mom."

My teenage son's room might not be perfect each day, but having it in order at the week's end is a reasonable trade-off I can live with.

Leverage in conjunction with veiled threats often works quite well.

"We're raising your allowance by $10 because we know how hard it is to keep your room in order. Don't worry, though, if you find you don't have time, the extra money spent for the housekeeper's time at $15 an hour can be deducted from your allowance."

In spite of the compensating increase in allowance, the financial responsibility usually has a definite impact. Once received, money is often hard to part with for this age group and can be an effective incentive.

In addition to money, teenagers also respond well to use of the car, dating privileges and curfew.

All I Want for X-Mas is My Two Front Teeth

Children are no longer singing this song. There is definitely a reason. They want BIGGER things. More toys to jam into their already packed little bedrooms.

There are usually two times a year when young children expect to receive presents. Their birthday and the holiday season. Prior to these occasions, it is a good idea to clean out the old clothes and toys to make room for the new. The anticipation of the upcoming event will help to inspire the anxious, young recipient.

152

Soliciting Help

It makes more sense if everybody in the family pitches in to get the job done then if just one person does.

Try establishing an early Saturday morning two- or three-hour ritual of quickly getting the house in order, so you can get on with enjoying your weekend without the cloud of guilt looming overhead.

When family members know precisely what is expected of them, they are more apt to keep things picked up during the week. If their Saturdays are especially important to them, they might even get their work done by Friday night.

We have six in our family. If everybody works together for just two and a half hours, that makes a total of 15 man hours, which is roughly the equivalent of two work days for a single person. When everyone works together, results are quicker and a more positive attitude prevails.

Respect Your Children

When you give your children presents do you let them keep their gifts or do you decide when it's time to pass them along or toss them?

When I hear parents talk about selling, giving away or throwing out their children's possessions I often wonder if they realize their unilateral decision shows disrespect to their children. If you give your child a present it should belong to him or her. I question our right to make decisions about their possessions.

Antique "nostalgia" shows are often filled with grown-up little boys and girls who attempt to recapture their youth by buying their favorite childhood toys that were tossed or lost.

If you have limited storage space, designate a reasonable area or large box in which each child can keep their favorite possessions and let them decide what is important to them.

Dweller Degree

I truly believe that you do children a disservice by not teaching them basic household skills. Taking care of oneself and environment should be acquired skills at an early age. By the time a child goes off to college, he or she should be well-equipped.

Here are some basics that should be learned:

- ☐ Make a bed.
- ☐ Wash a window.
- ☐ Wash a floor.
- ☐ Clean a bathroom.
- ☐ Shop for groceries.
- ☐ Put away groceries.
- ☐ Read a recipe.
- ☐ Fix a meal.
- ☐ Set a table.
- ☐ Wash and dry dishes.
- ☐ Load, operate and unload a dishwasher.
- ☐ Shake a rug.
- ☐ Vacuum a room.
- ☐ Pretreat, sort and put away laundry.
- ☐ Run a washer and a dryer.
- ☐ Iron a shirt.
- ☐ Sew on a button.
- ☐ Sew up a seam.
- ☐ Care for a pet.
- ☐ Wash a car.
- ☐ Plant a tree.
- ☐ Build a birdhouse.
- ☐ Paint a room.
- ☐ Wrap a present.
- ☐ Write a thank you note.
- ☐ Balance a checkbook.
- ☐ Change a diaper.
- ☐ Mail a package.
- ☐ Jump a car battery.
- ☐ Pop the clutch.
- ☐ Change a tire.
- ☐ Read a map.

Military Secrets

In boot camp the entire troop is held responsible if just one person does not perform adequately. Social pressure is the catalyst for maximum performance. It works.

I do not advocate turning your household into another Paris Island Military Training Camp; however, by making all parties responsible for daily maintenance, everyone will eventually recognize the importance of picking up after themselves. Habitual offenders are recognized as such and, pardon the pun, straighten up their acts.

Free the Slaves

It really isn't fair if just one person is responsible for keeping everything in order all the time. Resentment builds and, to make matters worse, the other members of the household start taking that person more and more for granted.

Eventually, that one person becomes a "personal slave." His or her total existence, or a large part of it, seems to be about picking up after others. How much better it would be if people would just pick up after themselves, so each person has more time to pursue his or her individual goals.

One way to cope with this common situation is to have a round-table discussion. Individuals can air their feelings and everyone can work toward a fair solution that incorporates clear responsibility.

One working mother greatly resented being the one who worked through the weekend catching up on the housework while her husband played golf and their two teenagers skipped out the door sports and social activities each weekend. Anyone confronted with such an unbalanced social situation can't help but feel bitter and resentful.

My suggestion was to reserve the first two hours each Saturday morning for completing household tasks together. Each of the four family members working for two hours is the equivalent of eight man hours or one work day. The wife and mother would be spared sacrificing her day off.

With all family members pitching in, members of this family could all get out and enjoy their different activities. With clear definitions of their responsibilities, they eventually found that some family members completed their tasks earlier in the week – or even on the previous night – to get a jump on the day.

Castles

Our ancestors had to work hard and long to be able to provide shelter for their families. Their homes were their "castles" and their scant furnishings were their prized possessions. They took great pains to care for their valued belongings, and these heirlooms were passed along from generation to generation.

Today we live in a modern world where consumer goods are taken for granted. When we tire of them we toss them and purchase better and newer models. When we lose respect for our homes and our possessions we are less likely to care for them. People often treat their homes like hotel rooms – a place to sleep, shower and change clothes and escape from.

When you appreciate and care for your home and possessions you beautify your surroundings and are more apt to enjoy the time you spend there.

Family Nesting Survival Skills

Often times its not that family members aren't willing to help with daily chores, its just that they don't "see" what needs to be done. However, to the person who routinely undertakes the bulk of the housework these same tasks appear obvious.

To aid in defining routine daily household maintenance, make a copy of the list below for family members. Have them review the list and put a check mark by the task they customarily do. When everyone is finished, tally and compare the results, then discuss whether it appears to be an equitable arrangement.

Afterward, go through the list again, line-by-line, and discuss who can take on more responsibility. Have each person edit their original list in a different color pen by putting check marks by the chores he or she is capable of doing. After a week, review the lists and discuss the results. Progress might be slow initially, but in time, these simple household tasks should become second nature to all. Remember, it's everybody's home and everybody should treat it with respect.

Bedroom:
☐ Make bed
☐ Hang up clothes
☐ Straighten room
☐ Relegate dirty clothes to hamper
☐ Remove items that don't belong

Bathroom:
☐ Clean sink after use
☐ Wipe off counter top after brushing teeth
☐ Clean mirror
☐ Clean toilet or at least wipe with Clorox disinfectant wipes
☐ Clean shower while showering
☐ Clean surface under shampoo bottles and soap dish
☐ Remove hair from drains
☐ Spray walls of shower with Tilex or squeegee shower glass
☐ Rehang mat
☐ Rehang or replace towels
☐ Return things to medicine chest, drawers and cupboard
☐ Refill toilet paper
☐ Rearrange towels
☐ Remove clothes

Kitchen
☐ Wipe table and counters
☐ Empty dishwasher to set table or put away as per plan
☐ Set table
☐ Prepare or at least start dinner
☐ After dinner:
    ☐ Return condiments
    ☐ Return unused utensils and place mats
    ☐ Store leftovers
    ☐ Rinse dishes and load in dishwasher as per plan
    ☐ Clean:
        ☐ Table

      ☐ Sink
      ☐ Counter top
      ☐ Stove top including burners
      ☐ Oven
      ☐ Microwave's five inside and one outside surfaces
      ☐ Refrigerator door and handle
☐ Organize contents of refrigerator
☐ Prepare refrigerator and pantry for Costco trip
☐ Unpack groceries
☐ Downsize containers for more refrigerator storage
☐ Break down boxes
☐ Store grocery bags and shopping bags as per plan
☐ Keep bins presentable
☐ Refill soap dispenser
☐ Refill water jug
☐ Make juice
☐ Add item to shopping list when used
☐ Feed pet(s)
☐ Take out garbage and recycling
☐ Replace compactor/garbage bags

Laundry
☐ Pretreat soiled clothes
☐ Hang dirty wet clothes to dry
☐ Put clothes in hamper
☐ Sort laundry
☐ Read washing instructions on garments
☐ Adjust water temperature
☐ Start washing machine
☐ Remove and hang permanent press clothes
☐ Adjust drier setting
☐ Start drier
☐ Fold clothes
☐ Put clothes away properly

Garage
☐ Make repairs
☐ Return tools
☐ Return gardening items
☐ Return sports equipment
☐ Return paint supplies
☐ Move garbage and recycling out on pick-up day

Miscellaneous
☐ Get newspaper and mail
☐ Change light bulbs
☐ Vacuum floors
☐ Wash floors
☐ Dust furniture
☐ Water plants
☐ Walk dog
☐ Clean pet cages
☐ Wash cars

Errands
☐ Do errands
☐ Call home for last-minute shopping list on way home

Returning Home
☐ Put away backpacks, keys, jackets, hats, etc.
☐ Put things in their proper rooms
☐ Take mail to desk

Snacks
☐ Make extras for other family members
☐ Wrap and store food
☐ Clean up kitchen

Homework and Projects
☐ Do homework
☐ Clean off work area

Television
☐ Organize video items
☐ Do small tasks during commercials

Leaving a Room
☐ Take things with you that belong in other rooms

Preparation for Tomorrow
☐ Prepare coffee maker
☐ Set breakfast table
☐ Set out:
    ☐ Keys
    ☐ Glasses
    ☐ Purse
    ☐ Jackets

☐ Hats
☐ Umbrellas
☐ Backpacks containing homework
☐ Lunch box supplies
☐ School lunch money
☐ Briefcase
☐ Errand list and related items
☐ Grocery list
☐ Outgoing items and receipts

Cruising the House
☐ Return out-of-place items
☐ Arrange pillows
☐ Straighten rugs
☐ Level pictures
☐ Clean off tables and surfaces

Final Clean Up
☐ Turn down thermostat
☐ Turn off lights
☐ Lock doors

Bedtime
☐ Set out clothes
☐ Set out cosmetics

Someone to Watch Over Me

When we're children we do our homework, study and pass tests to graduate to the next grade. When we're adults we work hard for our employers or we won't get a paycheck. However, when we procrastinate in our private lives there's usually nobody there that we have to answer to.

Become your own task master. Ask yourself what it is that stops you from completing it then try to overcome your mental block by break your project into a series of manageable tasks so it's not overwhelming.

Focus on the positive aspects of finishing your project and remind yourself how much less stress you'll experience. Make a to-do list and experience the satisfaction of crossing off tasks with a giant marker. Work toward regaining space. Getting back in control improves your self esteem.

Different Avenues of Learning

Not all of us go down life's main street to get where we want to go. Different people learn in different ways. Many take the direct route, others take the scenic detour, and the rest of us get lost several times before we finally reach our destination.

> *In addition to this book (reading), I have incorporated several media to further teach my organizing theories – my classes and lectures (audio) include several illustrations (visual) and demonstrations (tactile) while my in-home/office consultations (audio, visual, tactile) provide specific examples (watching, doing).*

Some of us learn by going to school and others achieve mastery by practical experience. Be aware of your vehicle of choice, whether it's learning by reading, watching or doing. Once you understand the easiest way you learn, focus on that avenue of learning and get to your organizing destination in record time.

The Dilemma

With the escalating cost of living, many couples are compelled to have two incomes. When both people work full-time, it seems only fair that they share equally in all of the household chores.

What if the amount earned by the primary wage earner is significantly highly than that of the spouse's income? Should the difference be reflective of their contributions to the household maintenance?

What about when one income is sufficient, but both choose to work? If one's work is elective, is it any less significant?

And what about the parent who doesn't work but stays at home with the children? Does that job stop at 5 pm.? Does one have a twenty-four hour job, or is there a sharing of responsibilities during the balance of the day?

There are no easy answers to these questions. These are issues which should be privately discussed until there is a meeting of the minds. If both parties are honest and caring people with a joint desire to have an orderly home, then the basic ingredients are there. Don't think in terms of giving 50-50, but rather of each party giving their 100%.

The Lion Trail

If your world is a jungle, perhaps it because you're following behind the lion of disarray on life's trail. Get beyond and stay ahead of your beast and you'll avoid having to watch where you step, and get to your destination faster and with less stress.

When you have constant clutter to address it impedes your progress and delays your success. Take time now to resolve unfinished business and remove guilt-laden obstacles to achieve your goals.

Loose Ends

Like an unmended sweater that soon unravels, our lives quickly fall apart when the tiny holes in our organized day are not promptly closed up.

I make a concerted effort to tie up as many loose ends each day before I retire. If I defer my minor projects too long, they tend to grow in size.

So, mend your little organizational snags and keep the fabric of your life intact.

Trivial + Trivial + Trivial = Major

Keeping a household running smoothly is a lot like treading water. Little things have a habit of adding up and, if you don't keep those legs moving, you're sunk. I prefer to think of these little things as:

Household Quicksand

Sink full of dishes
Half-eaten knishes
Shoelaces undone
Dry cleaning unhung.

Laundry on bed
Little doggy unfed
Missing game pieces
Pants with three creases

Timer is dinging
Telephone's ringing
Spill on the floor
Mail through the door.

Vase that just cracked
Groceries unpacked
Table unset
Diaper is wet.

Sweater needs defuzzing
Wash machine buzzing
Dinner party at six
I'm in a fix.

I considered myself fortunate to have had the luxury of being able to stay at home with my children and work out of my home at my convenience.

Occasionally, however, I'd daydream what it would be like to put on nice clothes with clean shoulders (no spit-up stains from babies), drive silently to an office, sit at a toyless desk without anyone sitting in my lap, type on a computer with no little fingerprint smudges on the monitor, peacefully sip hot coffee, without worrying about spillage, read a newspaper uninterrupted on a break, and occasionally have meaningful conversations with other adults and, incredibly, get paid at the end of the week – while others pick up toys and clean my house.

But, of course, if I had it over again, I still would choose staying at home with my children!

Seize the Moment and Just Do It

Greedily seize blocks of time. If possible, devote an entire day to tackling a room or two. Get an early start, put your phone on answering, ignore the doorbell and have a pizza or Chinese food delivered for dinner. If you don't take any breaks, you can avoid having to get started again.

So, sip your soda while you work if you get thirsty or have a cup of coffee to help you keep going, but work late into the night to finish what you started.

163

Turn that knob, open that door, enter that messy room you've been avoiding. Empty that desk and refill its drawers with what you already know belongs there. Sort those papers, then file them logically in labeled folders.

Let that closet spill forth its contents upon you and sort, sort, sort.

I take advantage of these times to slap a fresh coat of white interior latex paint on the walls. It doesn't take long, the brush cleans up easily with water and the room will be cleaner and brighter. A high-wattage light bulb can surprisingly resuscitate a closet and make it appear larger.

Before you refill your closet, think about what you want to store there and what configuration of shelves, poles or cabinets you'll require to make the best use of space. Simple shelving is a minor improvement – with possibly major benefits.

Anyone can build shelves with just a tape measurer, saw, hammer and nails. A stud finder will help you determine where your studs are located behind the sheet rock. More than likely, the 2 x 4 framing is spaced 16" from the center of one vertical stud to the center of the next stud.

However, by studying your existing shelf supports, you can usually follow the nails vertically in order to secure your 1 x 4s to the wall for the shelf support. The line of sheet rock nails can often be faintly seen running from floor to ceiling.

Measure and cut shelves, or take a shelf to the lumber yard and have them make duplicates. Turn any existing warped shelving upside down for a stronger shelving and to make it more esthetically pleasing.

Finding the Time

A common complaint is, "I never seem to find the time." The solution: Use your time better. Delay other activities and get your life in order first. Use the activities you postponed as rewards for your completed tasks.

Challenge yourself to get certain jobs done within a minimum amount of time.

> *I find that I am more organized if I have more to do. I can get a lot more done in one hour if I am under pressure; if I'm not under time constraints, the same tasks can take twice as long.*

> *To get a project finished early, sometimes I'll pretend the deadline is sooner than it actually is.*

Weekends are a great time to catch up on household tasks. A few hours every Saturday morning is a small price to pay for achieving a feeling of well-being and peace of mind for the rest of the weekend. For motivation, promise yourself something fun to do in the afternoon or evening.

Burning the Candle

In my estimation, twenty-four hours is too short for a day, but nothing can be done about it. The only real alternative is to use each day's time more wisely.

> *Like a rabbit escaping its hole before the sand truck dumps its load, I get up an hour or two before the children allows me to enjoy my morning coffee, read the newspaper, shower, dress, straighten my room and do a few little chores before the rest of the family arises and life's daily little trials begin.*

> *I don't get tired at night because I keep my energy level up by staying active. I find that if I do sit down and relax, my energy quickly wanes, especially after a meal or watching a television program.*

> *When I manage to keep going, my internal time clock prefers staying up till midnight – but, once in bed, I love having between eight and nine hours of sleep at night. If I succumbed to such a long rest, I would miss half the morning. So, I sacrifice some sleep most mornings to rise early, then try to catch up occasionally on the weekend.*

Hold Those Puppies

Maintaining order over the multiple aspects of your life is like controlling a dozen frisky puppies in the park. You wouldn't venture there without holding twelve leashes firmly in you hand. Likewise, keep a short tether to each of your responsibilities and keep a firm grip on them. By having control over your environment, you'll feel more in charge when life's wild dogs snap at your heels.

Making dinner when our children were ages six, four, two and newborn helped me master multi-tasking.

Hard Times

It is very common for a person who has lived through the Depression or had financial uncertainty in their life to develop a pack rat mentality. It's understandable that such an individual would tend to hold onto things for security. Many people who struggled in our early years continue to do so out of habit even after they've achieved financial security.

To overcome unnecessary frugality, remind yourself that life is to be savored and that you've earned the right to enjoy it.

Too Much of a Good Thing

Enjoy your possessions, but always in moderation. Be aware of the point of diminishing return on your investment when your collections grow and are left unchecked.

According to William Booth of The Washington Post, "the operator of a self-styled cat rescue mission" was found to have 589 cats inside her rental home. The chief veterinarian of the Department of Animal Regulation in Los Angeles recalled, "The floor was literally moving. It was all cats."

What might begin as a fond attachment can potentially grow beyond reasonable management. Just because you enjoy one thing doesn't insure you'll get twelve times the enjoyment if you possess a dozen more of the same.

The Golden Years

Often times people envision how much time they'll have to finish all their unfinished projects when they retire. Invariably, when they do finally reach their retirement years, they tend to take life a little slower, develop new interests, and find that they still don't have enough time to address unfinished projects. People who have accumulated a lifetime of "papers and things" need to make difficult and often long-deferred decisions. I truly believe that it is of utmost importance for seniors to quickly resolve these nagging issues so that they can get back in control again, achieve peace of mind, and begin enjoying the golden years they so richly deserve.

The Best Requested Bequest

When we fail to keep ourselves organized on a regular basis, our state of disorganization eventually grows to unwieldy proportions. Coping with everyday life becomes frustrating and resolving our clutter issues can be a major undertaking. Inability to get control of our possessions while we're young and healthy is compounded when we're older and limited in our physical and perhaps mental abilities.

People who delay organizing themselves before they become physically or mentally unable, move to a retirement community, or die leave their loved ones with the enormous undertaking of dealing with their possessions. Quite often their children are at a point in their lives where they're still struggling with careers and raising a family, and the added task of an estate liquidation further compounds their already hectic lives.

Trying to settle a disorganized parent's estate can be a long and painful process. It's like trying to solve a large jigsaw puzzle without benefit of the box cover. You must examine each piece of the puzzle and then slowly piece them together before you know what the "big picture" is.

Second Generation Procrastinators

Because children learn by example, children of parents with pack rat tendencies often repeat the cycle. On the other hand, if children perceive their parent's habits as a negative aspect in their lives, they often become ruthless in clearing their homes and offices of clutter for fear of becoming like their parents.

Children who have fostered their parents' procrastinating habits are more likely to let their parents' estate liquidation drag on indefinitely because of their inability to make decisions. Their feelings of helplessness and being out of control might compound the already-difficult mourning process.

The Battle of the Bulge

You know you've lost the battle of the bulge when you resort to renting storage units. When you opt to do so you, in essence, "buy back" your precious mementos with the rent you pay and often fail to realize that you are unable to see and enjoy their presence in your life.

Puddle Sitting

Don't wallow in self pity. Decide now if you are going to be a let's-just-sit-here-in-this-puddle-and-feel-sorry-for-ourselves type of person or if you're going to be a let's-get-up-and-do-this-that-and-the-other-thing type of individual.

Upon reflection, large projects usually don't turn out to be nearly as daunting as they usually appeared.

Psycho Babble

Time and money spent psychoanalyzing why you don't want to do the work necessary to get organized might be better spent with a professional organizer.

Many clients comment on how unexpectedly quick, easy and fun it is to get organized. Getting the organizing problem solved first, then learning how to maintain your home or office second, might be a better way to achieve your organizing goal.

Imagine your car engine breaking down into all its separate pieces. Would you sit and ponder the meaning behind why you don't want to reassemble it? Or would you hire a mechanic to fix it and then have him or her teach you how to maintain it?

It is What It Is

Sometimes things are precisely what they appear to be. Instead of seeking psychiatric or psychological avenues for some abstract or profound truth to explain why your possessions are disorderly, perhaps the answer is the obvious fact that your effects are disorderly simply because you haven't put them away. Its not unlike Freud's observation with regard to the symbolism of a cigar in a dream: "Sometimes a cigar is just a cigar."

Talk is Cheap

Don't waste precious time talking about your project. Dig right in and get started. All the time you squander discussing and mentally doing work would be better spent getting a portion of the job done. Be verbally and mentally economical and you'll be richer for it.

Keeping Afloat

Staying organized is like surfing. It's much less work to ride the cusp of a wave than it is to be caught inside it. Constantly strive to keep balance.

The Nutshell

The key word to success is:

Desire

The operative words are:

Willingness to work, solicit help and/or hire help

The general rule in organizing anything is to:

1. *Empty*
2. *Sort*
3. *Organize*

Determine the most logical place to put each group of items. Start with the largest things and work down to the smallest.

Your Ultimate Goal: Point Zero

Imagine what your life would be like if everything was in its proper place. What if you never again had to expend energy floundering around trying to locate something or trying to regain control of your life? Wouldn't it be wonderful if everything you needed was at your fingertips where and when you needed it? If you're completely organized, when life's big waves upset you, you'll have a better chance of staying afloat.

Close your eyes and envision the unfettered space within your walls. Visualize how much easier life would be if you were organized. Think about the peace of mind you'll have.

This is Point Zero. Get there!

SPACE-SAVING
REMODELING IDEAS

- CHAPTER XIII -

SPACE-SAVING REMODELING IDEAS

These are some ideas you may want to consider when talking to your architect or contractor before you renovate your home or remodel a room or two:

Activity Closet

• Waist-high, 3/4-deep shelf to act as writing surface, with stool in front

• Slightly-raised shallow shelf for colored pencils, crayons, markers, paints and brushes

• Multiple overhead shelves for coloring books, drawing paper, stencils, board games, cards and puzzles

• Overhead light fixture

• Recessed lower shelf for backpacks, lunch boxes, thermoses and water bottles

• Storage below for balls, helmets, roller skates, skateboards, and other sports equipment.

Baby Changing Closet

• Waist-high, full-depth shelf with two-inch lip at front edge and two-inch foam pad

• Multiple overhead shelves for diapers, diaper supplies and clothing

• Overhead light fixture with shade for baby's eyes

• Musical mobile suspended from ceiling or existing closet pole

• Shallow shelf below for extra diaper boxes and diaper bag

• Remaining space for diaper disposal, baby backpack, stroller, and other baby-related paraphernalia

Bathroom

- Raise height of counter to increase cabinet and drawer space below

- Cabinet with drawers of increasing depth from top to bottom in remaining cupboard space to house personal items. (See page 71.)

- Pull-out rack under sink to accommodate bottles and larger supplies

- Tip-out under sink for tooth brushing supplies, or hair brush and comb

- Maximum-length and -width mirrored medicine cabinets above sink with adjustable shelving and end doors opening inward for styling hair

- Recessed box in counter top with drop-down lid with electrical outlet in bottom to house two small appliances (hair dryer, electric curlers, curling iron, flat iron, or electric razor)

- Electrical outlet beneath sink for Dustbuster

- Position toilet behind short or full-length wall for privacy

- Toilet paper dispenser and matching storage unit between studs

- Tall, narrow, shallow cabinet(s) in wall between studs to store medicine (See page 70.) and surplus bathroom supplies

- Telephone

- Intercom

Bedroom

- Seating area for reading, private conversations, special breakfasts and cocktails

- Morning coffee bar in wall shared with bathroom for plumbing access

- Full-size display cabinet hinged and opening to secret storage room

- Recessed cabinet in wall with electrical outlet for recharging cell phones

Bedroom Closet

- Secret facia drawer with magnetic lock for jewelry

- Secret tip-out window sill bottom trim for small valuables

- Secret flip-out door finger molding side trim for small valuables

- Secret facia cupboards with press-release locks for gun storage

- Six-foot brass chain attached to top of wall by an eye screw for storing slacks on hangers suspended from every other link

- Laundry sorter access through wall shared with laundry or laundry-sorting closet

- Cabinet with slide-through drawers accessible also from laundry room for storing clothing

- Slanted dowel pegs on unusable wall for clothes, hats, purses or shoes

- Cabinet with multiple deep, tip-out drawers to keep shoes off the floor, dust-free, and at arms length

- Shoe shining kit inside step stool to access upper shelves

Computer Closet

- Bi-fold closet doors open to computer shelf with:
  - two-drawer file cabinets holding up desktop shelf
  - pull-out keyboard drawer
  - shallow shelf for small office "tools" (See page 128.)
  - shallow shelf for computer disk storage
  - cubbies for small office supplies (bank endorsement stamps, calculator, cards, disks, envelopes, stamp and tape dispensers, stapler, sticky notes)
  - literature sorter (See page 118.)
  - multiple overhead shelving for reference material, software literature and books

- Store full-size copy machine inside closet

Craft Closet

- Built-in sewing machine cabinet with overhead cupboards for fabric and lower cabinet doors below with storage boxes mounted to backside of doors for notions; hollow cabinet to house foot pedal and stool with removable seat to store divided rows of thread

- Pop-up cabinet to house sewing machine; cupboard doors below with storage boxes mounted to backside of doors for storing sewing notions

175

- Cabinets with adjustable shelving for fabric and large supplies

- Multiple shallow drawers for notions and small craft supplies

- Narrow but deep vertical cabinets for:
  – poster board and other comparably-sized items
  – plans and other tube-encased items

Den

- Back-to-back bookcases in adjoining rooms to give illusion of thicker walls

- Floor-to-ceiling bookcase with cupboards and drawers below and secret facia cupboard with press-release latch above for valuables

- Window seat with cushions and pillows above:
  – tilt-top cabinet
  – built-in bookcase
  – front-opening cupboard

- Bi-fold closet doors open to computer shelf with:
  – multiple overhead reference shelving
  – horizontal and vertical sorters for various papers and projects
  – two-drawer file cabinets below
  – tickler files accessible by hinged lid set into desktop. (See page 116.)
  – cubbies for small office supplies (bank endorsement stamps, calculator, cards, envelopes, stamp dispenser, stapler, sticky notes, tape)
  – shallow drawer for office "tools" (See page 128.)

- Partners desk in center of room with adequate space to accommodate The Baker's Dozen. (See page 112.)

- Murphy bed in wall disguised by framed artwork

- Chair-and-a-half-wide sleeper and ottoman to house pillow, sheets and blanket

- Built-in file cabinets or hidden safe recessed within wall behind hinged painting or display cabinet

- Surplus office supply storage in closet or cupboard

Dining Room

- Illuminated glass shelving recessed within wall to display crystal, china or a special collection

Display Cabinet Closet

- Change a small closet into a display cabinet; replace the center panel of the door with beveled glass, add glass shelves and an overhead light

Doorways

- Instead of closing off an old doorway make it into a shallow display cabinet for small items (See page 42.)

- Change room purpose by changing doorway orientation

- Create illusion of thicker walls by installing bookcases in adjoining rooms back to back

- Move door of bedroom off hallway to open onto entry to convert bedroom into an office

Entry

- Out-of-sight storage for keys, cameras, film, gloves, hats, mittens, purses, scarves and umbrellas

Garage

- Peripheral cabinets with gaps for opening car doors

- Recycle receptacles for cans, glass, paper and plastic

- Storage platform extending over car hood

- Overhead hinged storage boxes with catch latches between rafters for lightweight item storage

- Overhead platform above rafters for long-term storage

- Workbench with pegboard for small tools, organizer for hardware, drawers for supplies and shelving or cabinets for larger items

- Gardening area with provisions for tools and supplies located by door nearest yard

- Sports area with equipment racks and closet or trunk for sports-related clothing and accessories

- Picnic, pool and beach paraphernalia area

- Closet for out-of-season clothing

- Long-term storage area for holiday decorations, suitcases and old tax return files

- Surplus generator for power outages

- Built-in vacuum cleaning system

- Surplus pantry with secondary refrigerator or freezer

- Emergency/disaster supplies

Gift Closet

- Cupboard above for storing gifts and postage scale

- Clear counter for wrapping gifts

- Multiple wide, shallow drawers below for storing rolls of giftwrap, gift bags, folded boxes, tissue paper, ribbon, bows, tape, stickers, scissors, and package mailing supplies

Hallway

- Framed picture to disguise fuse box

- Crown molding shelves to display pictures or books

- Recessed cabinet between studs to display paperbacks

- Recessed cabinet with glass shelving and overhead lighting between studs to display collectibles

- Holes in top of hall linen cabinet counter for laundry sorting

- Laundry chute from second floor to laundry room

Kitchen

- Sink in center island with fixtures at side to allow access from either side

- Refrigerator and freezer "drawers"

- Cabinet with face frame between studs to display and store attractive spice jar sets, tea tins and antique canning jars filled with pasta, rice, beans, and dried food

- Vertical appliance pantry with pull-out shelves with multiple electrical outlets in rear for toaster, blender, mixer, breadmaker, etc.

- Shallow interior boxes on upper cupboard door interiors for small item storage

- Cabinets extending to ceiling for maximum storage and minimum dust collection

- High counters to ease back pain and provide more drawer and cupboard space

- Stepped counter for appliances to avoid crumb migration with optional roll-top enclosure or pocket door fronts

- Deeper than usual counter tops to accommodate equipment and/or decorations as well as providing work space

- Double half-round shelves attached to lower corner cupboard door fronts to access dead space in cupboards not large enough for a lazy Susan

- Pull-out table-top drawer with fold-out legs for extra work space or eating area

- Cookbook bookcase built into end of cabinet

- Shelf over kitchen window or doorway to display cookbooks or kitchen-related objet d'art

- Hole in top of cooking island or tilt-front facia for trash basket or recycling with accessibility below through cupboard

- Tip-out in front of sink and cook top for sponges and scrubbing utensils

- Baking center (See page 62.)

- Electrical outlet under sink for Dustbuster and rechargeable flashlight

- Trap door under sink flush with floor for disposal of broom sweepings with plastic collection container beneath flooring maintainable by periodic vacuuming or access from crawl space

- Dumb waiter to basement garage

Laundry

- Five laundry bins in cabinet with either vertical drop-front doors at top of cabinet front, or five holes in top of cabinet for sorting laundry for:
  – white
  – light
  – dark
  – towels
  – dry cleaning
  (Purchase plastic containers first to determine size of cabinetry.)

- Open-topped sorter for tossing laundry above washer and dryer area with hinged bottom to channel dirty laundry into washing machine

- Multiple drop-front doors on outside wall for laundry bin access between studs for depositing white, light and dark clothing, towels and dry cleaning with cupboard access inside laundry

- Common wall with master bedroom closet with laundry chute and sorter and two-way drawers for clothes and/or towels

- Drawers for sewing repair jobs, mismatched socks, rags and charity items

- Position sink next to washer and install dowel for hanging and drying wet clothes; disguise pole with facia

- Install decorative, notched shelf above washer and dryer to provide area for decorations, help disguise plumbing and electrical outlets and make machines' knobs appear recessed and less visible

- Laundry cabinet between washer and dryer to extend folding surface and keep cleaning supplies at accessible height

- Built-in ironing center

- Install telephone

Linen Closet

- Linen cabinet deep enough to accommodate depth of folded towels and sheet sets, and wide enough for folded blankets and comforters, and pillows (avoid excessively deep linen closets where towels and sheets are stored two deep and inaccessible)

- Electrical outlet for Dustbuster and rechargeable flashlight

Mud Room

- Cabinet for long coats next to separate cabinet for short jackets with multiple drawers beneath for car keys, gloves, mittens, scarves, purses, cameras, film and umbrellas

- Drying closet for wet raincoats, boots and umbrellas

- Cabinet with multiple shelves for slippers and shoes

Pantry

- Shallow cupboard set into inside of door which opens independently to house mop, broom and dustpan

- Boxed shelves on door interior for spices or small items

- Shallow shelving between studs for other small items such as spices, food coloring, cake decorating sprinkles, cupcake liners, packaged sauce mixes and jello

- Drawers for storage for pasta, rice, dried beans, grain and other plastic-wrapped dried food

Pantry Recycling

- Hinged door outside pantry wall for recycling with accessibility inside pantry

- Can cruncher mounted on wall above recycle bin

- Recycle chute from pantry to garage or basement garage between studs in wall for paper, plastic and aluminum (not glass)

Stairway

- Random steps to open for valuables and other candidates like gifts and gift wrapping supplies, telephone books, video tapes, in-house tools, lighting supplies (light bulbs, batteries, flashlights, candles, matches) or entertainment (cards, poker chips, board games, etc.)

- Short, diagonal-top door in hallway to access storage area under stairway for luggage or vacuum cleaner

The Ever-Changing Closet

Newborn to Toddler:
• Convert clothes closet to baby changing closet

Toddler to Twelve:
• Convert former baby changing closet to craft closet

Twelve to Twilight:
• Convert former craft closet to:
  – computer closet
  – display cabinet
  – gift and gift wrap closet
  – media closet
  – office supply closet
  – project closet
  – repair closet
  – sewing closet
  – surplus pantry
  – wet bar, if closet shares wall with existing plumbing

Walk-In Closet

• Knock out back of closet and make adjoining closet a walk-in closet

• Knock out wall between two back-to-back closets to make one walk-in closet accessible from both rooms

• Knock out back of a deep closet and divide space with adjoining room

Wet Bar

• Hook up to existing plumbing in wall from adjoining room for a wet bar

Wet Bar Closet

• Convert closet that backs up to plumbing into enclosed wet bar

Chapter XIV

Dear Granny Noodles . . .

Dear Granny Noodles: My sock drawer is a mess. I can never find a matching pair. How can I organize them?

Matchmaker, Matchmaker: Make them a match. Night after night in the dark they're alone, so make them a match to call their own.

After pairing up all the lonely little mates, fold each happy couple over twice, slip the top single layer of the cuff back around to form their own little sleeping bag and tuck them in tightly right next to each other.

Newly married socks prefer segregated little campsites with nice rows of blue, pink, white, etc., campers.

Mixed marriages are frowned upon in the sock world. Single socks must wait at the back of the drawer in Sock Limbo until their mates return from serving time in the Laundry Corps. If they are found to be missing in action, then their mates must be transferred to Rag Bin Detail.

If your fingers refuse to cooperate, roll each pair up and put it in a sock organizer, available at household organizational shops. Some look like honeycombs and others resemble checkerboards, but either style will provide individual partitions in which to place your socks.

Socks live happily ever after in these special little homes.

Dear Granny Noodles: Help! My garage is like a three-ring circus. Something is always going on there and I don't know where to look first. I can never find what I'm looking for.

Stop! Don't send in the clowns! You are not at the circus. If you take a closer look, you'll see that you're actually in your own little personal hardware store.

Imagine that you are going to open for business in two days. You need to organize and display your wares.

Begin by separating items into specific departments. You'll have hardware, tool, lumber, electrical, plumbing, garden, pet, and sports equipment sections. Start with the section with the largest boxes and equipment and choose convenient locations. Seldom-used items need to be stored then put them up and out of the way, perhaps in the rafters. Work your way down to medium-sized items then to smaller items. Finally continue on to the next department.

Old dressers and cabinets can provide storage as well as work surfaces. Consider the benefits of nailing a plywood platform over rafters and installing a pull-down stairway.

Present your merchandise in logical order while making it as visually attractive as possible.

You'll be in business in no time!

Dear Granny Noodles: My adorable, sentimental wife brings so much junk into our home that I have to walk sideways to get from room to room. She won't part with anything. What should I do?

Dear Mr. Rat: Your wife has a severe case of Pack Rat Syndrome.

Please understand that no slight is intended in referring to your wife as a small rodent; however, it is undeniable that your sweet, nostalgic little mouse is habitually collecting and bringing various debris into your nest. Oh, excuse me, home.

The initial symptoms are high paraphernalia intake and low decision-making ability. Symptoms are compounded by confined spaces and, if not treated, eventually result in paralysis. Yes, victims of this disorder have been known to surround themselves until, in the final stage of the syndrome, they become completely immobilized.

Pack Rat Syndrome is more commonly known as Shrinking Nest Phobia. Moving into a larger nest merely delays the inevitable, and is not recommended as a cure-all.

Know that you are not alone. Many people suffer from this affliction. Some people have been known to survive this debilitating illness but it takes a strong will, a concise prescription or plan, and a definite block of time for recovery.

Dear Granny Noodles: Our eight-year-old son absolutely refuses to clean his bedroom We cannot walk across the floor of his room without stepping on his many little toy collections.

Dear Mr. and Mrs. Gulliver Travels: Surprise your son with another collection – a collection of handsome boxes or baskets.

Sit down on the floor with him and make a game of sorting his toys and putting them in their own special place. Let him help decide which shelf will house each toy basket.

If he begins to lose interest, don't panic. Calmly say, "That's okay. Just pick up the ones you want to save. Little Billy Bratt down the block can have whatever you don't want." This usually brings immediate results.

Another favorite is, "Just do the best you can. The Vacuum People will pick up the rest later." This, too, has been known to work wonders.

Start with the largest toys and store them on bottom shelves or on the closet floor. Reserve easily accessible shelving for smaller items and store seldom-used articles on the upper shelves. For toddlers, store small items out of reach; take one basket down at a time for use and return it immediately after playtime.

The lesson to be learned here is that if everything has a home base, The Battle of the Little People is over.

Dear Granny Noodles: How can I better organize my medicine chest? I'm forever replacing soggy emery boards and rusty scissors. I have enough medication to open a pharmacy and my tubes are all squeezed-out.

Dear Drug Junky: I have the perfect plan for rehabilitation for you.

Group medication together by kind to avoid duplication. You will be able to determine at a glance what you have on hand for each symptom such as:

> Allergy medication
> Antacids
> Cold and flu medication
> Cough drops
> Decongestants
> Eye drops
> Nasal sprays
> Pain relievers
> Prescription
> Vitamin supplements

Designate another area for first aid, which includes Ace bandages, adhesive tape, anesthetics, antiseptics, gauze pads, and, of course, Snoopy Band-Aids for those really bad cuts.

Use an old coffee mug to hold wet toothbrushes and razors. A second mug can hold tubes of cream and toothpaste, with a third mug for all your small metal items – like metal nail files, nail clippers, scissors, and tweezers which can hang over the side of the cup. Clean up your act!

Dear Granny Noodles: All year long I throw my receipts into one big box and, come tax time, I'm faced with one big mess. My tax accountant sends me a workbook to fill in the amounts but it seems to further complicate the process.

Dear April A. Teenth: Don't tax your brain any longer.

Measure the height of last year's tax receipts and papers and, allowing room for expansion, delegate adequate space in your filing cabinet for all related tax paraphernalia. If you don't have a filing cabinet use a small metal file box.

Look at the tax preparation workbook your accountant gave you last year. For each item total you needed to enter last year, label a manila folder. Arrange your manila folders in hanging folders labeled numerically to correspond with your accountant's workbook, page numbers and page content.

For example, a hanging folder might be labeled: Page 8 - Deductions. Inside will be four labeled manila folders containing all related receipts and papers:

> 8 - Medical & Dental
> 8 - Real Estate Taxes
> 8 - DMV
> 8 - Interest Paid

At the end of the year, just staple the receipts, record the totals and wait for your rebate!

Dear Granny Noodles: Whenever I try to organize my pantry, I can get my canned and boxed goods to look decent but my bags of pasta, rice, and other assorted bagged goods misbehave and always look unruly.

Dear Ms. Kay Os: Get control of those disruptive little criminals. Extradite them from the pantry system and put them in more secure confinement.

Incarcerate them within the four, walled sides of their own special drawer. Because they are restricted, they cannot easily escape.

Separate culturally diverse groups. Put Italian pastas together in rows. White, brown, Basmati, and even Lundberg rice interact well with wild rice. Keep the nuts away from dried fruit.

Make sure you can see all inmates. Don't let those pesky popcorn packages slouch. Make them sit upright at attention to make room for the packaged Oriental noodle soups.

Lock up inmates in secured, clear plastic enclosures where they can be easily viewed and tightly warehoused. All available space can be fully utilized. Only when they are granted superfluous space do they tend to become recalcitrant.

Let bagged goods serve their time well in your kitchen. As a reward for good behavior, you might even get out early!

Dear Granny Noodles: We have many little collections that we would like to display and enjoy, however we can never get them to look attractive. How can we achieve that decorator's touch?

Dear Producers: Lights, camera – Wait! Hold everything! I can't see all the actors.

As in any stage production, it is imperative that the viewing audience be able to see the main characters clearly. Actors are egotistical by nature and will become impossibly difficult if they feel they're being upstaged by lesser actors.

Decorating any stage is really quite simple. Begin with your star performer. Position this proud character upstage to compliment your set.

After strategically placing this focal point, consider your supporting cast. Finally, fill in the gaps with your extras. Never position one actor directly in front of another. Each egotistical little player wants to be seen and heard.

By all means, give each production its own theme. You'd never find a cartoon in an Elizabethan play, a newscaster in fiction, or a rock star cast in a nature series. Cast related actors in productions that fit their characters.

Remember these little tricks and all your shows will be picture perfect!

Dear Granny Noodles: My daughter is forever leaving her blow hair dryer on the bathroom counter and I'm getting tired of always having to put it away for her. I'm also very concerned about the danger of leaving an electrical appliance near a water source. How can I get her to pick up after herself without nagging her every day?

Dear Blowing a Fuse: Avoid the electrocution concern by installing a dedicated safety circuit. Any contact with water will immediately disconnect the fuse.

As for the ever-present hair dryer, its a known fact that a teenage girl's fragile brain is wired to disconnect when told what to do by her mother. The only way this circuit can be overridden is by rerouting the verbal request through her telephone. Unfortunately, it's virtually imposssible to translate common English words into a language and simultaneously imitate her best friend's voice.

Impromptu singing is your only other alternative. I highly suggest a couple hearty verses of:

The hair dryer goes in the drawer
In the drawer, in the drawer
If you put it back in its place
I won't sing this song anymore
No, I won't sing this song anymore!

There is scientific evidence that such high-decibel singing permanently blows out daughters' fuses.

Dear Granny Noodles: Help! am forever getting stranded by the gentlemen in my family who never replace empty toilet paper rolls before they leave the bathroom. No matter how many times I complain, they never courteously replenish the supply.

Dear Wanda B. Dry: Those are not gentlemen. Gentlemen have consideration for women and would never leave one stranded on a porcelain island.

Don't depend upon on your brood of unthoughtful brutes for simple acts of kindness any longer. Forget turning them into princes and store your bathroom tissue supply within arm's reach of your throne.

Tear out a 5-inch wide, 30-inch vertical section of sheet rock between the studs of the wall, next to your toilet, and install a toilet paper cabinet. You'll be able to store a package of 6 rolls inside. A 10-inch wide cabinet will hold a dozen rolls.

Inside the unit, attach a clear plexiglass panel in the middle section to secure the bathroom tissue. Leave 5 inches open at both the top and bottom for loading and unloading the full rolls.

Build this clever dispenser so that the next time you find yourself out of paper, you won't be out of luck. Just open the cabinet door, retrieve a new roll, replace the empty and keep on rolling!

APPENDIX

The Daily Planner

Copy the form on page 194, or just memorize the outline, and use it every day. It enables you to identify and list the four realms of work — telephone calls, appointments, errands and projects.

Vehicle Service Record

Attach a copy of the form on page 195 to the front of each car, van, truck or motorcycle file to use as a summary sheet to reflect repairs, dates, the shop names and mileage.

> *Since we have a number of vehicles, it's difficult to remember which car got what tires and when, the date of each last oil change and the warranty period for each battery, etc. By using this cover sheet for each car's yearly receipts, I can see all the information at a glance.*

Because most repair receipts record the car's odometer reading, I can easily calculate my yearly mileage for tax purposes.

DAILY PLANNER

Telephone Calls

Telephone Number	Name	Notes

Appointments

Time	Name	Notes

Errands

Time	Name	Notes

Projects

_____

_____

_____

_____

_____

_____

VEHICLE SERVICE RECORD
for

_____

(year and make of car)

Date	Mileage	Improvement	By	Cost

Tip-Out Drawer
Construction Diagram

To make this clever little drawer, first remove the decorative cabinet panel in front of any sink, then add a three-inch bottom, two-inch back, two curved sides and two hinges to join the bottom edge of your existing cabinet.

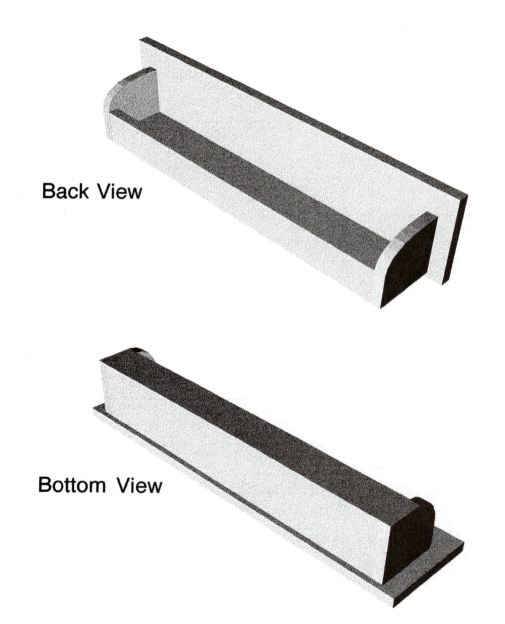

Back View

Bottom View

Student Survival Kit

Every student needs to be prepared with the tools of his trade:

- ☐ Computer
- ☐ Printer
- ☐ Large desk
- ☐ Comfortable chair
- ☐ Lamp with good lighting

- ☐ Almanac
- ☐ Atlas
- ☐ Assignment book
- ☐ Dictionary
- ☐ Thesaurus

- ☐ Pens
- ☐ Pencils
- ☐ Colored pencils
- ☐ Crayons
- ☐ Markers

- ☐ Erasers
- ☐ Glue stick
- ☐ Hole punch
- ☐ Paper clips
- ☐ Pencil sharpener

- ☐ Rubber bands
- ☐ Scissors
- ☐ Stapler and staples
- ☐ Tape dispenser and tape
- ☐ White out

- ☐ Computer paper
- ☐ Construction paper
- ☐ Graph paper
- ☐ Lined notebook paper
- ☐ Tracing paper

- ☐ Binders
- ☐ Index cards
- ☐ Page dividers
- ☐ Report folders
- ☐ Sheet protectors

Finding Misplaced Money

Are you absolutely certain that you haven't lost or misplaced assets, tax refund checks, insurance policy benefits, savings bonds or money which rightfully belongs to you or is just waiting to be claimed? If you're in doubt, below is a list of agencies you might contact to verify if any funds are being held for you or your family members:

AMERICAN COUNCIL OF LIFE INSURANCE
1001 Pennsylvania Avenue N.W., Suite 500
Washington D.C.   20004-2559
(202) 624-2000 or FAX: (202) 624-2319
– *regarding unclaimed insurance benefits* –

CALIFORNIA STATE CONTROLLER'S OFFICE
www.sco.ca.gov
– *regarding various funds* –

CALIFORNIA UNCLAIMED PROPERTIES DIVISION
Post Office Box 942850
Sacramento, CA   94250
(800) 992-4647
- *regarding unclaimed properties* -

IRS - SPECIAL PROCEDURES DEPARTMENT
(800) 829-1040
– *regarding uncashed tax refund checks* –

THE FEDERAL INFORMATION CENTER
(800) 688-9889
www.info.gov
– *regarding any other questions* –

THE FEDERAL RESERVE BANK
P. O. Box 419440
Kansas City, MO   64141-6440
 (800) 333-2919
– *regarding uncashed mature savings bonds* –

HOLOCAUST CLAIMS PROCESSING DEPARTMENT
New York State Banking Department   2 Rector Street
New York, New York   10006
(800) 992-4647 within the U.S.
(212) 618-6983 outside the U.S.
– *regarding over 3,000 Swiss banks accounts holding Holocaust victims' money belonging to the rightful owners or their heirs*

What to Throw Away and When

Automobile reports and claims of settled cases – 7 years
Accounts payable and receivable ledgers and schedules – 7 years
Audit reports of accountants – Indefinitely
Bank deposit slips – 7 years
Bank reconciliations – 7 years
Bank statements – 7 years
Bank electronic fund transfer documents – 7 years
Canceled checks for tax deductible major purchases – 7 years
Canceled checks for non-tax related items – 7 years
Canceled checks for tax, property or contract payments – 7 years
Cash books – Indefinitely
Chart of accounts – Indefinitely
Construction documents – 3 years after sale of property
Contracts and leases – 7 years beyond expiration date
Contribution records – 7 years
Correspondence of importance – Indefinitely
Credit card records – 7 years
Deeds, mortgages, bills of sale, title – Indefinitely
Employee personnel records – 7 years after termination
Financial statements for end-of-year – Indefinitely
Health records – Indefinitely
Home-improvement expenditures for capital gains taxes upon sale of property – Indefinitely
Home purchase and sale documents and each IRS Form 2119 – Indefinitely
I-9's – 1 year after termination
Insurance policies – 3 years after expiration
Inventories of products, materials, supplies – 7 years
Investment records – Until sold
Invoices to customers – 7 years
Invoices from vendors – 7 years
Journals – Indefinitely
Licenses – Indefinitely
Loan documents – Until paid off
Minutes books of directors and stockholders meetings, including by-laws and charter – Indefinitely
Notes receivable ledgers and schedules – 7 years
OSHA logs – 5 years
Payroll records and summaries, pensions, payroll taxes – 7 years
Petty cash vouchers – 3 years
Property appraisals by outside appraisers – 3 years after sale of property

Property records including costs, depreciation reserves, end-of-year trial balances, depreciation schedules, blueprints and plans – Indefinitely
Purchase orders – 7 years
Receipts for major purchases should be attached to their warranty and instruction booklets
Receiving sheets – 1 year
Sales records – 7 years
Scrap and salvage records – 7 years
Subsidiary ledgers – 7 years
Tax returns and worksheets, agents' reports, documents relating to income tax liability – Indefinitely
Trademark registration – Indefinitely
Voucher register and schedules – 7 years
Vouchers for payments to vendors and employees including allowances and reimbursement for travel and entertainment expenses – 7 years
W-4 forms – 4 years
Workers' compensation documents – 11 years

Consult your lawyer or accountant regarding the variation of rules in your industry, locality or state. The above-mentioned retention guideline may not necessarily be deemed accurate.

What to Keep in a Safe-Deposit Box

Adoption papers
Appraisals for antiques, home, jewelry and special collections
Birth certificates
Custody agreements
Deeds of trust
Divorce decrees
Family tree history
Household inventory
Insurance policy/agent list (also keep copy of documents at home)
Marriage certificates
Passports
Photo negatives (most valuable ones)
Stock and bond certificates
Wills (keep a copy as your lawyer keeps the originals)

Whereas others offer 12-step programs,
because of Pack Rats Anonymous' mastery of efficient use of time and resources,
we are able to offer you a 9-step program:

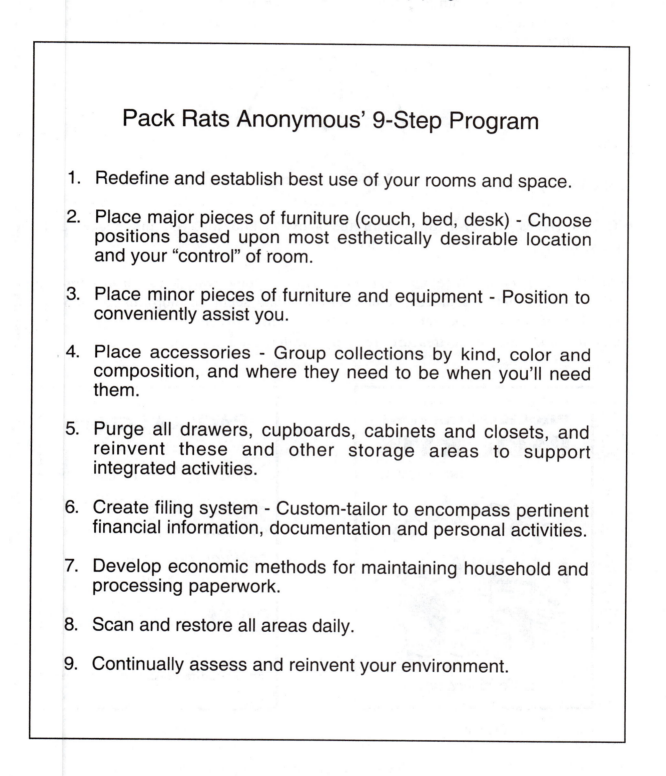

Pack Rats Anonymous' 9-Step Program

1. Redefine and establish best use of your rooms and space.

2. Place major pieces of furniture (couch, bed, desk) - Choose positions based upon most esthetically desirable location and your "control" of room.

3. Place minor pieces of furniture and equipment - Position to conveniently assist you.

4. Place accessories - Group collections by kind, color and composition, and where they need to be when you'll need them.

5. Purge all drawers, cupboards, cabinets and closets, and reinvent these and other storage areas to support integrated activities.

6. Create filing system - Custom-tailor to encompass pertinent financial information, documentation and personal activities.

7. Develop economic methods for maintaining household and processing paperwork.

8. Scan and restore all areas daily.

9. Continually assess and reinvent your environment.

BECOME A "PACK RATS ANONYMOUS" MEMBER!

Join thousands of other Pack Rats Anonymous members and get back in control of your life. Visit **www.packratsanonymous.com** and learn about club membership and available services.

Membership includes:

• Cotton Hanes' Beefy-T Shirt with the above subtle logo on the pocket and the pack rat logo and code on the back:

• Membership card. Whether you carry it in your wallet as proof for those, "I've got to get organized!" conversations that seem to pop up all too often, or give it to a pack rat friend with a sense of humor, this clever plastic membership card is a treasure for any wallet, bulletin board or picture frame.

(front)

PACK RAT CODE:

"In the fight to combat the chaos of chronic clutter, to eliminate the heartache of habitual hoarding, and to avoid the perils of paper paralysis."

www.packratsanonymous.com

(back)

Need a professional organizer?
Call our nationwide, toll-free referral service at 1-877-7PAK-RAT.

Notes:

Notes:

Notes:

Notes: